I AM SOMEONE

SOMEONE

AISLING

CREEGAN

Gill Books

Aisling Creegan is an artist who has degrees in Fine Art, and Counselling and Psychotherapy. She lives in Wicklow. You can see Aisling's paintings on the New Irish Art website, or through her @creegan.studio profile on Facebook or Instagram.

Aisling has put together a list of organisations that can support people affected by the issues she has written about; this can be found at the back of the book.

Gill Books
Hume Avenue
Park West
Dublin 12
www.gillbooks.ie

Gill Books is an imprint of M.H. Gill and Co.

© Aisling Creegan 2022

978 07171 9374 5

Designed by Typo•glyphix
Edited by Sands Publishing Solutions
Proofread by Emma Dunne

Printed by Scandbook AB, Sweden
This book is typeset in 13 on 18pt, Adobe Garamond Pro.

All rights reserved.
No part of this publication may be copied, reproduced or
transmitted in any form or by any means, without written
permission of the publishers.

A CIP catalogue record for this book is available from the
British Library.

5 4 3 2 1

I dedicate this book to those of you who might have gone through difficulties in your own childhoods and who might continue to struggle with their legacy today. I hope you will find something here to give you strength and a reason to carry on.

CONTENTS

Part Three: A Certain Freedom

PROLOGUE

THIS BOOK STARTED AS A DIARY, just for me to mark my own journey. Sometimes, it's only when you see something written in black and white that you realise the enormity of it. I knew that my childhood hadn't been easy, but writing about the brutality and fear that were inflicted upon me then made me understand that I'd been through so much. Even so, after sitting down to write two or three chapters of this memoir a few years ago, I suddenly became self-conscious, threw them in a drawer and left them there. A couple of years later, I was telling my story to a friend, and she said, 'You know, you have a story to tell, Aisling, and it's your duty to get it out there.' It was as if someone had turned on a light switch. I realised that it wasn't about me now: it was about helping others. That was the push I needed.

In January 2020, I contacted one of my primary school teachers. Máire had thrown me a lifeline as a child, providing me with a safe space to begin to flourish, and I'll never forget what she did for me. Being able to thank her at long last made me realise that now was the time to get started. When Covid struck, being in lockdown gave me the chance to reflect on my life, take stock and open those diaries again. This book took shape during a period in isolation in the early stages of the pandemic.

During that time in isolation, the words just seemed to flow, as I realised that the story had been inside my head all along. The other thing that spurred me on was the fact that my partner, Susan, was so encouraging. Without her support, it could have taken me a lot longer, maybe years, to write this book. While I was in isolation, Susan would request a new chapter to be read to her through the bedroom door each evening. This really motivated me. That – and the fact that she kept throwing bars of chocolate into the bedroom!

As the child of alcoholics and as the daughter of a woman with poor mental health, my childhood was one of violence, of the kind that a child should never witness. Many times as a youngster, I felt that there was only one option for me: to kill myself. I kept a razor blade, safely wrapped in greaseproof paper, in case I couldn't go on. I never slept more than four hours a night as a child, in case my mother, or one of her drinking buddies, would attack me. This habit lasted into adulthood, and it's only in the last few years that I've felt safe enough to get a full night's sleep.

My mission as a child was to stay alive until the next day. When I went to school, which I didn't very often, I was always fascinated to see classmates chatting about pop stars, TV and fashion. There was no jealousy on my part: I just couldn't relate to it. It was as if I'd gone from being born to immediately becoming an adult. Picking up broken objects and washing blood off the kitchen walls before going to school wiped out any thought of childish ways. The descriptions of terrifying physical and sexual assaults in this book may be hard to read at times, but they were important for me to write to understand the girl that I once was and how far I've come.

There is also humour here, and my spirit as a child is still visible. I loved the outdoors, nature and playing around with the neighbourhood kids, even if I had to make my own dinner when I got home. I always held the belief that we are born for a reason. And if I'd had a book like this to read as a teenager, it probably would have helped me to understand that I wasn't alone and would have given me more strength to carry on.

That's why I'm writing my story. If I can touch just one person who is struggling in life and has thoughts of suicide, then laying my soul bare in this book will have been worth it. I could so easily have become an alcoholic myself, ended up addicted to drugs or homeless. I was a witness to the devastation that alcohol could wreak, and I knew that I didn't want that for my own life. I don't know if I could put my finger on any one intervention or support that saved me, but the fact that I didn't go down the same road as my parents, that I survived my childhood and lived to tell the tale, has given me a mission to get this book into as many crisis centres as possible.

My family and friends are going to read details of my story for the first time, and I'm very aware that this may open some wounds. I don't know what experience my siblings had, because we have never spoken about it, but I can only write from my own perspective.

As a society, it's only now that we are talking more openly about mother-and-baby homes, sexual assaults, physical assaults and so on. Even so, in Ireland, we still tend to have that 'Sure, that was in the past' attitude. It may be in the past, but the fact is, the body never forgets, right down to the cellular level. There are people walking around today who bear the scars of the things that happened to them as children, and while counselling is extremely helpful, no amount of therapy will ever get rid of traumatic memories. All counselling can do is help us to come to terms with what happened.

For me, there's also the question: do these events shape who we are? I think in my mother's case, they most definitely did: as a young woman, she endured a trauma that undoubtedly contributed to her alcoholism and poor mental health, all the more so because it was brushed under the carpet. In my own case they also did, to a certain degree. I went to college, held down a job and met the love of my life, but things could just as easily have had a very different outcome. I've had plenty of setbacks along the way and could have thrown in the towel many times, but each time I felt that my will to keep going was weakening, the little Aisling in my heart would lead the way.

While I dearly loved my father, and I believe he loved me, I have to say that I never had any feelings for my mother, because I couldn't relate to her. I have no memory of Mammy hugging me as a child or speaking to me tenderly. I had seen other parents expressing affection towards their kids, so I knew that something was terribly broken in my relationship with Mammy. There just seemed to be no bond between us. As a very young child, I was more confused than angry about this.

Believe it or not, I wanted to call this book *You Are Nothing*, because that is what my mother would say to me when I was a child, over and over. Later in life, I decided to reframe her criticisms with positive statements, so that I could understand that they weren't true.

'YOU ARE NOTHING.'
You are everything, each cell, every molecule, root and bud.
'YOU WERE NEVER ANYTHING.'
You have always been present, ageless, timeless, flourishing and building momentum.
'AND YOU WILL NEVER BE ANYTHING.'
Accept all of nature, shedding, renewing, bending, splitting, healing. Your fingerprint is yours alone. You are unique. Nothing can imitate you. Celebrate the very existence of you and burst through that bud.

PART ONE

MAMMY, DADDY AND ME

CHAPTER ONE

THE MANTRA

T IS 1977, AND I AM SEVEN YEARS OLD. My mother is standing over me, repeating her mantra over and over again. That I am nothing and never will be anything. To a young child, if you hear this often enough, it quickly becomes part of your psyche. It gets absorbed and embedded in your brain. Every single cell of your body feels the sting of those words. I just feel so old and worn out. I have two choices: to die or to hang on till I'm sixteen and old enough to leave. I get such comfort from the thought of dying. Imagine... no more fear of my mother's rages, no more fear of her sudden changes in behaviour. I actually can't picture it. And when I imagine the nine more years until I can leave, it's just too much. I can only break it down into blocks of 12 hours. It's day by day. If I can make it through until tomorrow morning, I'll take it from there.

I have absolutely no control over anything except my belongings. The surface of my dressing table is completely taken up with tiny figures and other gadgets that would seem meaningless to anyone else. They don't hold any sentimental value to me, but they are a constant. I can rely on them. Figurines, animals, Matchbox cars, all strategic-ally placed, never moved. They are there in the morning and in exactly the same place at night. There is a thick layer of dust on the table's surface, but they cannot be disturbed. I can't open a window in case a breeze will knock over one of my treasures. My bed is like a tabletop, completely smooth, because I can't seem to tolerate crinkles on the blankets. I can't sit on the bed because I will disrupt it. It's as if I'm trying to control things as best I can, at least at the start of the day. Who knows what will have happened by the time night comes.

By the way, my name is Aisling, Ais for short. I come from a large Dublin family, and we live in a comfortable home on the outskirts of the city. There were once seven of us, but my sister Noelle*, who would have been a year younger than me, died of cot death when she was an infant. I don't remember her, but I miss her presence des-perately. My brother Enda, who at four years older is nearest to me in age, has a mild learning disability and is in residential care, even though he stays with us

---

* All names of my siblings are pseudonyms.

sometimes. I wish Noelle was alive, because my mammy terrifies me. If Noelle was here with me, maybe we could protect each other. Mammy was 42 when she had me, and there's a big age gap between me and my other siblings. My older brother Sean is busy working and he's not here that much, while my sister Clare is nearly finished secondary school. My two eldest sisters, Louise and Maria, have already left home. I can't wait to be older so I can get away from this house and stay away as much as I can, especially at the weekends. That's when most of the drinking and fighting happens.

I'm a very short, skinny, dishevelled-looking thing, mischievous. Apparently, I'm quite funny. I don't intend to be: it just comes naturally to me. I give myself a bath once a week and I muck around a lot in gardens and tree houses, just like every other kid of my age. But I also bite my fingernails until they bleed. I have a fascination with tearing their cuticles. I always have at least two fingernails infected, with green pus on the cuticle. I find the searing pain to be a distraction from the other stuff going on in the house. Punching the wall with my fist is also a favourite distraction of mine. The wall is solid, so I'm not heard. I get such relief from it.

At this age, it's hard to say how I'm feeling. In general, I'm quiet and live very much in my imagination. I draw constantly, the sun always present in every picture. There are always vast landscapes with rolling hills, rivers and

birds, horizon after horizon. I escape into these landscapes and swear that if I survive, I will live among these
rolling hills.

I can't stand concrete, traffic, constant noise. These
things make me uneasy, because I need to concentrate as
hard as I can on the noises inside the house, to figure out
the atmosphere. Big trucks flying by disturb that concentration. I can't read or write, and I don't know my
address. I hardly go to school, and there doesn't seem to
be much of an issue made of it, either. The days are mostly
spent playing with my Action Man and Matchbox cars.

I have this routine where I place an old Matchbox car
on the ground and imagine my mother is in it. I hate my
mammy, because she hurts Daddy and he's sick. I place
the car on the ground and climb up on top of the coal
shed. I drop a big heavy stone on the car. I get this euphoric
feeling every single time I do it. I keep running out of cars!
Action Man gets it too. He is my prisoner, and the torture
he receives is very much dependent on how my day has
gone. In general, his hands get tied, I slit his side with a
razor blade and bury him alive for a couple of days.

It never occurs to me to wonder what this seven-year-
old is doing with a razor blade. I have it neatly wrapped
in greaseproof paper under my bed, in case I do want to
die. The option is always there.

CHAPTER TWO

COMMUNION AGAIN

TODAY, IT'S 27 MAY 1978. I made my First Holy Communion recently. Mammy said if I wear the dress again today, I might get another few bob from the people drinking in the pub, but I don't care about money. This dress feels so alien to me. It's not that it's fussy: I just don't wear dresses, because I'm a bit of a tomboy. I like climbing trees and messing around in the fields around the back of the house with the neighbourhood boys, like Dave and Ger.

While Mammy and Daddy are in the pub, still celebrating my Communion, I'm mooching around the back of the pub car park. There's a building site there. Now I'm happy. I'm doing plenty of exploring, in spite of the dress. Then I find a trowel and I'm delighted. I start digging into the soil, thinking that Daddy's going to be happy with this, because we don't have a trowel. Maybe one day he'll make something with it. As I run into the pub to tell him about my discovery, I'm trying to brush some of the dirt from my dress. They seem somewhat oblivious to my find due to the fact that they are all drunk. There's nothing new about this, so I exit the scene and throw the trowel on the seat of the van through a gap in the window.

With nothing else to do, I'm back inside. The hours pass, and I feel so bored. I hate sitting inside the pub, but it's getting cold outside. Darkness falls, and I'm resigned to sitting with them. The alcohol has piled up on the table. Cigarette smoke is thick in the air, and there are drunken men bellowing out rebel songs. I can't stand it. They're getting seriously drunk, and I'm feeling sick to my stomach. *Why the hell did I have to have a Communion?* I think. It's just another excuse for my parents to get hammered. Mammy and Daddy are like two powder kegs, ready to explode at any minute. I hate going to pubs with them, but Mammy orders me to go, so I've no choice.

At last it's time to go and we get into the van. I'm in the back. Before my mother settles into the passenger seat, I lean in and quickly move the trowel so she doesn't sit on it. I close my eyes and pray. It's a two-mile drive to our house, and I hope we'll make it without something happening. Here we go. She screams at him to watch where he's going, because he's weaving all over the road.

I'm on my knees in the back. I take my white clogs off since they're cutting into the back of my thighs as I crouch in the dark. We're halfway home. *Please God, please God,* I think, *nearly there.* The screaming and shouting grow more ferocious. Then Daddy lifts the trowel and smashes it across my mother's skull. This is the first time I've ever seen Daddy hit Mammy. Silence. He slams on the brakes, opens the passenger door and, with his outstretched leg, forces her body off the seat and on to the road.

There's more silence for a second, then the side door opens, and I'm yanked out, my clogs slipping off my feet. Mammy grips my arm with her wet hand, sticky with blood. Hysterical, she commands me to knock on someone's door to call an ambulance. All I can think is that I'm so embarrassed. I'm walking on a main road, barefoot, in a bloodied Communion dress. My parents' drunkenness is now public.

I get to a house with a wishing well in the garden. How ironic. I run up the front path and knock on the door. It could be the early hours of the morning, I don't know. When the door is answered, I apologise and ask if they can call an ambulance. My mother, of course, is falling apart, screaming at the top of her voice and being really dramatic, her arms swaying about in the air. I don't even feel concerned because it's happened so many times before. She could be dying, for all I know. Every weekend it's the same story: drink, screaming, blood. I feel numbed by it all. I'm mad at myself, really, because I was the one who put that trowel in the van. I feel totally exhausted.

We arrive at the hospital's Accident and Emergency department, and Mammy is wheeled away on a trolley in a bloodied state. We've been in this situation countless times, where Mammy has lashed out at Daddy in a drunken rage, but Daddy has never fought back until now. And while I can handle washing splattered blood from the sitting-room walls on a Monday morning after one of their binges, I get so embarrassed when other people see it.

Daddy and I sit on the hard plastic seats and wait. He's sobering up now, but he's in a kind of stupor. When I ask if he's okay, he just shrugs his shoulders and says nothing.

After what seems like an age, my mother, smelling like a brewery, is escorted back to us, the wound on her head stitched together. The nurse tells me Mammy's going to be fine. 'You look after her,' the nurse says as we leave the hospital. As hardened as I am by this carry-on, I do know it's not the way it should be. It's been going on for so long that it feels normal, in a strange way, but what scares me now is that the fights seem to be getting more ferocious.

CHAPTER THREE

WALKING THE CORNFIELD

T'S SUMMER NOW, AND MEMORIES OF THAT NIGHT in hospital have begun to fade. I'm on my holidays from primary school – not that you'd notice the difference, because I don't go to school that often. Mammy works all day, anyway, starting at her job for the health board before I'm even meant to be getting up for school. Daddy does cash-and-carry deliveries. Sometimes he lets me come with him. I love sitting up the front of the van with him, watching the streets and parks go by.

I stir in the bed. Give my itchy nose a rub. My neck is stiff from lying on Panda's leg. Panda is my co-pilot. Some kids suck their thumbs or carry a special blanket; me, I have Panda. He's about three foot tall and nearly as wide, big and soft. His thighs are my pillows. We have endless conversations, me and Panda. Sometimes, he seems like the only person in the house I can talk to.

The sun is casting the most amazing light on my wall. Every time I see light from the sun, I always imagine that it's coming from heaven itself and that an angel is descending towards me. I love this feeling, but I don't know where it stems from. I don't go to Mass, but I do pray to God when I'm afraid, and I always feel so bad about this, because I never seem to just talk to God when things are calm, probably because this is rare. There's always tension in the house, and I always feel that I need to be on alert.

It seems quiet. I think I'm the first one awake. Oh, yeah, stretch those arms and legs. I move my legs out to the edge of the bed and very carefully move back the curtains, so as not to disturb my little bits and pieces. Also, I don't want to wake *her*, because if I do, there'll be hell to pay. I sneak out to the toilet, put some toilet paper in the bowl first and have a slash, very slowly, so I don't make noise. This takes lots of muscle control, which I have down to a fine art. I don't flush. As I tiptoe past her room, I take a peek, making sure to avoid the creaky floorboards. I know each one by heart. The ones on the stairs are the worst. Yes! She's not there. She must be gone to work. No matter what the nights are like, Mammy always manages to get up for work. Daddy doesn't have to go to work till later in the day, which is good for him. He's always tired in the mornings and makes himself a glass of raw egg and milk – yuck.

I jump into my shorts, T-shirt and runners, and as I pass through the kitchen, I push my hand into a box of cornflakes, emerge with a fistful and stuff it in my mouth as I hasten down the back garden. I can't waste a second of this glorious day. I sit on the back wall and soak in the morning, the trees at my back, birds bursting with song and a seamless sky. This is heaven. I realise that no matter how bad my night is, the sun will still rise. I might spend my nights lying awake, afraid to move a muscle in case she comes into my room and starts screaming at me, or worse, but at the sight of a sunny day, I feel a sense of hope and freedom.

I see a couple of figures at the end of the lane. As they get closer, I realise it's Ger and Dave, two lads from the back of my road. They join me on the wall, the greeting a simple 'Hiya', after which we don't have much to say. Still, I get a good feeling from them, and their quietness is something I cherish. The lads are about two years older than me and, as we haven't been ravaged by puberty yet, there's still a great sense of innocence and equality to our relationship. There are no expectations whatsoever – none of that awkward stuff – and besides, I'm just like them: I like having adventures.

Today, the lads suggest going to Murph's field. I'm up for it, of course. I always am. Actually, there are a lot of fields belonging to Murph, a local farmer, but this is the one we go to most. This field is full of corn, hence the attraction. They say Murph has a shotgun, and rumour has it that he's tied children up and left them naked in a shed as punishment for going through his corn. These rumours don't concern me one bit. We jump off the wall in unison, the bricks chafing my thighs, and we saunter down the lane. We get to the back road and cross a second lane. We get there within five minutes.

'Wow, the colour,' I say. It's been a while since I was here, and I'm mesmerised by the sea of gold in front of me. We walk to the edge of the field and see evidence of previous explorers who have left their trail of destruction. I can't wait to dive in there. Ger suggests we take our tops off in the heat. Without hesitation, they're off. Jesus, the pure sense of freedom. For a moment, we just look at each other. We realise that one of us is a girl and she's almost naked, but she looks exactly like one of the lads, right down to the short hairstyle. Not that it bothers us. We venture forward on our journey, and I feel like I'm going to smash into pieces of excitement, being enveloped by this blanket of nature, the corn pronging my flesh and my body engaging, responding to all kinds of sensations. I feel so alive. At times we burst into laughter. No words are needed. We run, run and run faster. I'm sweating now, drops of it running from the base of my neck and down my shorts. My breastbone is glistening, and my forehead is beading. After a time, we stop and collapse in a heap. The sun is so hot now. We lie on our backs and look up at the sky. The heat feels like velvet on my face. We just lie there. There is no time. Time is for grown-ups who wear watches.

Suddenly, Dave jumps up. He startles me. He says he heard something. Maybe it's Murph. Maybe he is sneaking up on us and he's going to lock us in the shed. The adrenaline is starting to flow. We all raise our heads very slowly. I don't see anybody, but our imagination is starting to rev up. We begin to hear strange sounds, and when a breeze catches the corn, we convince ourselves it's Murph. The threat is titillating. This is adventure! This is the stuff of the Enid Blyton books that I see on the shelf in school and I swear I will read some day, because I can't yet, even though I'm almost eight. Anyway, for the time being, I don't need to know how to read. Apart from anything else, why would people want to read on a sunny day? When I go to the park, I see people with books, newspapers and magazines, engrossed as they sit slap bang in the middle of Eden. I don't get it. Maybe that's what all grown-ups do when they get big. I hope it doesn't happen to me. Mammy reads a lot. Newspapers and books, never magazines. She likes thick books with big titles on them. The only thing is, they're often used as missiles against Daddy. I'd give anything to have her read me a story, but she never does, and I'd be afraid to ask her, in case she'd lose her temper. I think that if I could read, I'd take better care of my books.

I get back out of my thoughts and realise that we were making up the whole scenario of Murph coming upon us. I guess we like to get each other going, to add to the excitement. Now we come up with a brilliant idea. We stick our tops back on. There's a shady area in the far corner of the field, under a canopy of trees. It's always mucky there, and we decide to play a game of 'let's see who can get stuck in the muck'. Delighted with our idea, we all make our way to the corner, which seems innocent enough but is filled with dark muck. Ger sticks his foot into the mud and keeps going until it's halfway up his shin. Then Dave wades in, followed by me. I start to have difficulty moving in it: I'm surprised by how heavy muck is. I've never walked through it before, but it quickly sucks my foot down. 'I just lost my shoe!' I cry. The imprint of my leg is still in the mud, so I pour my leg back into the cavity and eventually I feel the shoe, into which I gladly slide my foot. I'd be killed for losing a shoe, but the excitement outweighs my fear of the consequences.

Then I see that Dave has completely lost his balance – he's actually sinking. This isn't funny now. Dave starts to panic and cry. Ger and I make our way slowly towards him and pull at his arms, but Ger slips and I lose my grip. I decide the best thing to do is to get back on to the bank and give him a branch to grab on to. Between the two of us, we yank Dave out. Knackered and relieved, we collapse in a heap on the bank. We all got a fright there. Still, our parents will never know. To them, we've just been 'out', which is the way things should be.

Bang! The crack of the shotgun makes every bird in every tree around the field take flight. I run. I don't look left or right. I hear feet running behind me. I don't think I'm breathing, because I'm so scared. I remember all those stories I heard about Murph, and it dawns on me that this one's actually happening. My legs are weighed down by the wet soil. *Just focus and run*, I think. I notice there don't seem to be as many footsteps behind me, but I dare not look back. Then I'm aware of someone else coming up behind me. Please God, let it be Dave or Ger! If it is Dave, what happened to Ger? Did Murph catch him? Did he kill him? Will he be stripped and locked in that shed, like they say? *Run, just run!* I tell myself.

I'm coming out of the lane and flying across the road. There are no cars. If there were any, I'd be dead. My legs are getting weaker now, but I can't resist the temptation to glance over my shoulder. Oh, Jesus, Mary and Joseph, it's Murph, wielding a double-barrelled shotgun. He's catching up with me. I scale the back wall of my garden, and he flips himself over it after me. He must be in a rage to keep going like that. I just can't lose him. I dart to the back door. Just as I reach for the handle, Daddy swings it open. Thank God it isn't Mammy – if it was, I think I'd rather be in Murph's hands.

I fall against Daddy in exhaustion.

'Who are you running from?' he says, patting my head.

I say, 'Nobody,' just as Murph makes it to the door. He points the gun at me and orders my father to keep his 'son' away from his fields.

Daddy apologises, grabs me by the collar and hauls me inside, closing the door on Murph. 'Tiger,' he says, using his pet name for me. 'What did you get up to?'

I tell him about my morning with the lads, leaving out the bit about getting stuck in the mud. 'Ah, Tiger,' he says softly, draping his arm around me. He seems flat in himself. Then, suddenly, he smiles and says, 'Do you know what your first word was?' My ears prick up. Apparently, I was sitting on a potty in the kitchen. I lost my balance, toppling over with the potty, and I'm not proud to say that my first word on this earth was 'shit'.

'Off you go and clean yourself up before Mammy sees you,' he says. He winks at me, and we understand each other completely. We never know when Mammy might strike.

Mammy runs the washing through a mangle after she takes it out of the washing machine. The mangle has two huge rollers that squeeze the water out of the clothes, and when they come out like boards, it makes me laugh. The other day, though, Mammy grabbed my hand and tried to push my fingers towards the big rollers. 'You don't deserve hands,' she shouted. I started screaming, and she just laughed and let me go. She didn't even seem drunk.

I'd better get my clothes clean, and quick, before she spots them. I get a big bucket, fill it with water and soak the shorts, T-shirt and runners in it, run a bit of carbolic soap over them and throw them over the line. They'll be grand.

Later that evening, I'm lying in bed, thinking about my day. I realise that Murph had called me 'son'. He thought I was a boy! Wow, this gives me a whole new dimension. I really like the idea. I've always been looked on as a tomboy, but this is different. I feel quite empowered by my new status. It's not that I see girls as being weaker than boys, but I see boys as having a different kind of experience, a freer one. Come to think of it, all my friends are boys, except one girl, but she's dead on. The girls I know in school love to dress up in pretty dresses and wear clips and hairbands, which to me seem torturous, and they all tend to look like each other.

Sometimes, we're allowed to bring our pets into school, and the girls bring in their miniature dogs in baskets, with pink bows in place of collars. Sorry, but give me an Alsatian any day. A dog to me is a comrade, a pal you can roll around with and who'll put you in your place if you piss him off. Still, it's lovely to have a real dog in the classroom on special days. I'd love to bring in my dog, Scruffy, but she's a mongrel and looks a bit rough. I love her, but I think she'd scare the girls in my class.

I never thought about boys' and girls' roles before, but I do know I never want to get married or to have kids. Relationships, in my world, seem to be built on anger. At those so-called singsongs on a Sunday morning in the pub, the men and women of the family swing their arms around each other, but they seem hostile at the same time. There's nothing gentle about it: it all seems too much. Sunday is the day I despise most of all. Mammy, Daddy and I go to the pub early in the day, then we go home for something to eat and then it's straight back to the pub. They get tired and cranky from drinking so much, and if they don't fight, Daddy just conks out for the rest of the evening.

I can't help feeling that Mammy resents Daddy for some reason. I've never seen her being nice to him. How do we know that the person we spend our life with isn't going to hate us? Mammy seems so full of hatred. I think I would quite happily stay on my own when I'm older; all I need is a way of earning money to be independent. But because I rarely go to school, I find learning really hard, and I know that this isn't good. Even so, I never get bullied. Maybe I can hold my own better than I think. When I do go to school, I tend to do my own thing. In the schoolyard, I play chasing with others sometimes, and at other times I sit quite happily on my own. Being part of a group is not a necessity for me – I would describe myself as a bit of a lone wolf. I do enjoy interaction: it balances those times of pure loneliness, filled with trying to figure out what's happening at home.

I'm a curious child, I know, and I'm completely fascinated by our whole reason for being. Why are we here on earth, I wonder? Why are we surrounded by animals and nature, sunrise and sunset? Although I don't know why, I do know that the world around me gives meaning to my existence. I have such a strong belief that I'm here for a good reason. I just hope I find out what it is soon, before I crack up.

Maybe there will come a time, when I'm older, that I might like to have a partner. How would I trust them, though? How do you know for sure that your partner isn't going to beat or humiliate you, like my mother and father do to each other? I make a vow to myself, that when I am independent and I have a say, nobody will ever raise a hand to me. Being violent and scaring people to death is not the way it was meant to be. Somehow, I know this: God makes too much beauty for my life to be this unhappy. But no matter what happens in my day, the sun will always rise the next morning.

CHAPTER FOUR

A JOURNEY

T'S LATE SUMMER NOW, and I wake up, my eyes sticky with sleep. I can hear the attic beams cracking in the heat. I take a deep breath in. The sun is bursting through the window again. I just lie there, thinking about heaven and angels. I start to think about dying and wonder if it's painful. I've been thinking lately about the different ways people die, and I wonder if I'll die before I get big. Mammy makes me so afraid: when she throws things like knives at Daddy, sometimes they nearly hit me. Daddy legs it, and I take cover behind the furniture. I stay there until she runs after him, then I escape out the back door if I can, or hide in another room. Sometimes, I end up crouching down behind the sofa for a couple of hours until things calm down again. When it's quiet, I clamber back into the same shorts and T-shirt that I always wear, go to the toilet, then run downstairs. I can't wait to get out of there.

Today, before I get to the kitchen, I hear someone rustling around. My heart stops. Mammy must be in there. As I walk in, I see a suitcase just inside the door. Mammy looks up at me. 'Don't you go anywhere now; we're going to the train station.'

What is she talking about? I didn't know we were going away. I ask where we're going, and I'm simply told, 'Shut up.' That's that. It doesn't matter, I decide: it'll be nice to go somewhere on the train. I can't remember when I was last on a train. I think it was a couple of years ago, when we went to Butlin's in Mosney. I hate that venue: the chalets are like prison cells, and the singing from the bar, where my parents spend their time, echoes around the grounds like some horrible carnival.

I don't bother with breakfast because I'm kind of excited about this trip. It's a magical mystery tour, I decide. Thinking about it that way will make it easier. Mammy never tells me what we're doing, and I hate that: I need to know what's happening, because not knowing makes me more anxious that maybe the surprise at the end won't be a nice one. Within an hour or so, we're sitting on the bus. Mammy only has one suitcase and isn't as dressed up as she usually is when she's going somewhere nice. She's wearing her lipstick alright – she'd never leave the house without that – and her thick blonde hair is up in a perfect tight bun, but she's not wearing one of her good dresses. She looks like a film star when she's dressed up. Men and women often turn their heads when Mammy passes them. She's been told loads of times that she looks like Princess Grace.

When the bus conductor gives me my ticket, I roll it up and pretend it's a fag. There are loads of people smoking on the bus. Even though I'm fascinated, I hate when people don't open the windows to let the smoke out. The bus fills with thick smoke that burns my eyes. Mammy says nothing on the journey, but that's not unusual – she rarely talks to me. Suddenly, my hand is gripped and I'm yanked down the stairs. Why does she always have to grip me so tightly? When we reach the bottom of the stairs, she pushes me in front of her and sticks her fist between my scrawny shoulder blades to usher me on. We get off the bus. As we walk down the quays, the Phoenix Park – my sanctuary, the place where I've spent so many summer days climbing trees and wandering through the long grass – is straight ahead, and I look at it longingly as she shoves me along ahead of her to the train station.

I love the train station. The building is gorgeous, and I love the cool air rushing through on a hot day. After Mammy pays at the ticket office, she brings me, holding me by the wrist, to the train. Why won't she ever hold my hand? I've seen other parents holding their kids' hands. Why doesn't she do it? She says nothing as we walk towards the train. She places the case inside the door of one of the carriages. The man with the cap blows his whistle. It makes a shrill sound that seems to echo forever. The train jolts forward, and just as she lifts me on to it, I realise that she's not coming with me. She tells me I'm going to Granny's and that Granny will meet me at the other end. Then the door is shut, and the train starts to move.

My head can't register what's happening: I was so sure we were both going somewhere, but now I'm on a train on my own. How will I know when to get off? Where is the other end that Mammy spoke about? I'm only eight. I can't read, so the signs for the towns and villages that we pass through mean nothing to me. I feel terrified, like vomiting with fear. An inspector appears then and tells me not to move from this carriage. I can't stand this feeling of being helpless. If only I was old enough to work, I think to myself, like my brother and sisters, I could earn money and control my own life, but I'm too small to work, so I've absolutely no choice. I don't even know how long I'm going to Granny's for or why I'm going. But as I stare out the window, I notice that the sun is following me all the way from Dublin. If the sun and the birds come with me to the countryside where Granny lives, I know I won't be as afraid.

After ages, the train grinds to a halt. I jump to my feet. I must have dozed off. I was having another one of the nightmares I've been having lately. In these dreams,

I'm being chased, and when someone grabs me and forces me to stop, I try to speak, but words won't come out of my mouth.

Then I see a woman making her way towards the carriage. She steps on, leans towards me and tells me nicely to come with her. She seems kind of familiar to me, but I'm not really sure. I think she's one of my relatives from down the country, where Mammy's from. My head goes completely blank. I can't think straight, and my words are a jumble. The woman is asking me questions, and she seems friendly, but everything about this situation is unfamiliar, and that terrifies me. The woman leads me away from the station, my suitcase banging off my ankles, and we walk until we get to the main square of what looks like a small town. I don't know the name of it, but I don't need to. Grey houses, grey shops, grey sky, grey birds, until we stop outside my granny's home.

I don't remember ever meeting my grandaddy because he died a while back, and I don't see much of Granny while I'm here, because she always seems busy in the family business, a hardware shop. There's always lots of people in the shop. It's deadly: you can buy anything in it. The shelves are lined with boxes full of screws and nails of different sizes, and the paint cans are lined up according to colour. I love to look at them. While Granny's doing her work, I spend my days sitting on the pavement outside the shop, chatting to the gravel and the stones. I'm happy enough, playing in my own little world. I'm used to it. One Sunday morning at home in Dublin, when Mammy and Daddy were gone to the pub, I set myself up outside our gate with a box and asked the neighbours on their way to the church if they had any odds or loose change. I made a good few bob that day. If my mother had known, she'd have killed me. She takes great pride in being good with money, working hard and paying her bills promptly, and I know she wouldn't approve of me begging like that. I did it for the craic.

I don't know why I'm staying at Granny's. Daddy's in hospital with his breathing again; maybe it's something to do with that. I miss seeing the Wicklow hills from my bedroom window. I miss the cornfield, the park, the sun setting on the hills at the end of the day. And I miss Dave and Ger, and the effortless connection we possess. I have no idea what people are saying here because I don't get the accent, but I do enjoy the way it curls at the end. The lads here haven't given me any hassle. I kind of thought they would, me being from the Big Smoke and all. If someone did start on me, though, I wouldn't give in. A while ago, I got myself into a situation where I had to be hauled off this fella by two older men because he'd called me names. I wasn't happy making a spectacle of myself like that in public – I normally leave that to my parents – but it just hit a nerve. He was a lot bigger than me, which wouldn't be hard, but that didn't stop me. Mammy is always blaming Daddy and me for doing things we didn't do, and I feel like I've had enough of Mammy and her friends pushing me about. Maybe that's why I'm always ready to defend myself.

The days roll into each other, with me playing outside all day until I'm called in for my dinner, or tea, which is lovely. Nobody pays any attention to me here, but then nobody bothers me either, and it feels very different to life at home. I don't feel threatened here, and it's lovely to get a break from the screaming and shouting in my house.

Then the case is back in the hallway, and it's time for me to leave. Within minutes, I'm heading back to the train station. Oh, I'm excited. It's strange: as bad and frightening as things can be at home, it's still my home. I feel the natural world around my house holds it all together and makes it possible to bear what's happening at home. My wish, when I'm older, is to live in the hills of Wicklow, close to nature.

As I pass the same landmarks on the train going home, the anticipation beats in my stomach: was Panda safe in my absence? Did anyone disturb my room? I'm excited about seeing Mammy, too. I did miss her. I'm confused as to why, when she's angry with me all the time, but I just missed my mammy. I wish she was like my friends' mammies, laughing and talking with me and maybe even hugging me when I fall out of a tree and hurt myself.

The train grinds to its final stop. It's a lot colder these days than it was when I left Dublin. I stick on my coat and I see her. The doors are opened, and I pull out the case. She's standing on the platform ahead of me, not moving. I leave the case on the platform and sprint towards her. I call out to her, again and again, 'Mammy, Mammy!' and I run as fast as I can towards her. As I get closer, I open my arms, until eventually I make contact. I wrap my arms tightly around her and I hold her. She stands there, motionless, her arms limp by her side. I'm almost tearing at her flesh to get her to react, but nothing. I'm only short of pleading with her to acknowledge me, but she doesn't. She orders me to get my case, and as I pull it along, I see the back of her walking out of the station. I simply follow.

CHAPTER FIVE

HOME AGAIN

SCAN MY BEDROOM AS I ENTER. I have this need to know what's happening on every single surface, against every wall, underneath the bed and on my dressing table, where I keep my treasures. I have enough surprises in my life, and I need to control whatever piece of my environment I can. I notice that someone has disturbed my dressing table: some of the tiny figurines have been moved. I know this because the thick coating of dust on the surface has been shifted. I go into a rage and feel completely blinded by temper. I smash my bare fist into the wall, and tears pool in my eyes. At these moments, I can't even stand the sensation of clothing against my skin. If only I could crawl out of my skin altogether.

After a time, the pain in my knuckles calms me down a little. I feel that I can think again. I rearrange the figures, but it's so hard: for each one I stand up, another one gets knocked down. There's not one bit of empty space on that surface. Eventually, everything is put back exactly the way it was before, each piece strategically placed, just like in a chess game. These soldiers, clowns, cars, miniature Eiffel Towers, Dracula teeth, creepy crawlies and the contents of Christmas crackers are never to be moved again. Each one of them has its place. I don't question their purpose, only that I have set myself the task of caring for them.

At the end of each day, all my Matchbox cars have to be lined up neatly according to their size. I got a couple of new cars recently, but Mammy doesn't know. If she knew how I got them, she'd kill me. I had seen them in the local shop. I'd been looking at them for ages. Before I went to Granny's, I went back in and couldn't resist the temptation. The cars were displayed in their boxes on a shelf close to the shop entrance. I took two cars out of their boxes, then placed the empty boxes back on the shelf, got down on the floor and flicked the two cars out the door when the coast was clear. I then stood up, cool as you like, walked around the other aisle, came out the front door, picked up my two new additions and headed home. Where I got the neck, I don't know. I'd never done it before and I don't feel good about it, so I probably won't ever do it again.

I walk to the bathroom to run some cold water over my knuckles. I look in the mirror and notice that some hairs on the top of my head are standing up by themselves. I yank them out one by one. It's a sharp, sweet sensation. I go downstairs and make my way towards the kitchen. Mammy's in there. I watch her through a crack in the kitchen door. Today was the shopping day. Every surface is occupied by food. The radio is blaring out rebel songs, which make me feel uneasy. She's not the kind of woman to sing or hum gaily along with music. Sometimes this level of noise means she can be ready for an outburst, but at what level, I never know. Sometimes, she can lash out; at others, she can completely ignore me.

For Mammy, the big shop is not a simple case of putting away groceries, which should take maybe fifteen minutes or so: it's a military operation, with enough food to feed an army, even though there's only five of us in the house. Her mission is to sort through, separate, butcher and tag the meat, and there's a lot of it. Mammy loves meat. Some of it may be cooked now, then frozen for a later date. She's tearing at the mince with her bare, stubby hands, her nail varnish as red as the blood draining from the meat. She seems to revel in these shopping expeditions. This event happens every two weeks. It has an almost festive feel to it.

As I watch her through the kitchen door, I remember the Christmas when I walked into the kitchen to be met with a live turkey. I was so mesmerised by this beautiful creature, with its silvery-black feathers and wobbly red throat. The thought crossed my mind that maybe she'd brought this beauty home as a pet. The only other way I'd experienced turkey was on a plate. This gorgeous thing was nestled under my mammy's arms.

Mammy smiled reassuringly and beckoned me towards her, and as I came closer, I could feel excitement beating in my chest. I slowly reached out my hand to make contact with the turkey. I didn't want to frighten it and risk getting bitten. The turkey was looking at me with the most beautiful shiny eyes. At that very moment, Mammy flipped the turkey around and twisted its neck, slammed it on the countertop and hacked its head off. My arms were still outstretched. I was bolted to the ground.

Now, terrified by that memory, I bound up the stairs with no regard for the creaky ones, which I normally avoid in case she hears me. When I reach the top, I just halt. I don't know if I want to get sick or where to put myself. I go to my room, curl up with Panda for a few minutes and try to shut my senses off, especially my hearing. The radio is still screaming, 'The auld triangle went jingle jangle…' blasting through the house. I gaze out the window and watch the traffic passing. The sheer sense of freedom one must feel getting into a car and driving away – it's unimaginable to me.

I get up and make my way to the door, determined to go outside for some fresh air, even if it means I'll have to go through the kitchen and past Mammy. The rebel songs are still blaring away in the kitchen. I can't stand this music, because it reminds me of the Sundays when I'm forced to come along to those singalong sessions in bars and bear witness to the drunkards singing away. Fuelled by alcohol, for a so-called 'family' day out, it always feels out of control. Do they all go home in the afternoon and kill each other, the way my parents do? Or do they just fall into a stupor from all the alcohol they've consumed in such a short space of time?

I go down the stairs again. As I enter the kitchen cautiously, Mammy has her back to me. She's now in the process of beating the life out of some meat with a wooden mallet. She swings her arm back and crashes it down on the bloodied mess like she's missed her true vocation. I try to slither behind her to get to the back door, but just when I'm almost past her, she swings her right arm around her back and grabs me. Jesus, how did she see me? She looks at me with a gleam in her eye, and immediately I know she wants a little fun. Her kind of entertainment. I never know what it'll be, but I do know that it'll be painful. She tightens her grip and effort-lessly pulls my arm around towards her. The rest of my body just follows. She's quite short but heavy and dense, and her grip is powerful. I never stand a chance.

Before I know it, my right hand is on the chopping board. Before I can register another thought, the mallet crashes down on my fingers. I actually feel nothing. She bellows with laughter, and as I'm staring up at her, I notice a cold feeling in my fingers. I feel quite serene in my pain, and I don't even try to pull my hand away. The way I feel at this moment, she could break every single part of me, and I probably wouldn't even know it. After what seems like an age, I withdraw my hand and go to the back door. As I exit the kitchen, she just resumes where she left off, hammering and bashing the meat. Sometimes walking through that house with her in it is like walking through a field of landmines.

The pain is now searing through me.

Sundays are the worst days with Mammy, though, because she and Daddy start drinking early in the day and come home plastered by lunchtime. We've never gone to Mass like everyone else. Maybe Mammy and Daddy don't believe in God, I don't know. Anyway, it doesn't bother me not going to Mass, because I prefer to talk to God when I'm outside among nature.

Mammy and Daddy hardly talk when they're drunk, and I tiptoe around the house the whole time so she doesn't hear me, because she's always in a bad mood. I hate it when she screams and hits me whenever I try to help Daddy after she hurts him. The other night, she pushed him down the stairs, and he lay at the bottom, dead still. When I went to run to him, Mammy gripped me as hard as she could and wouldn't let me go. I wriggled out from her grasp and went flying down the stairs, tears falling down my face. I put my hand on his chest to see if it was rising and falling. It was. I was so relieved. Daddy then opened his eyes and looked at me wearily. Mammy was now halfway down the stairs, a big glass vase in her hand. 'Get back up here, or I'll break your skull,' she said to me. I had no choice but to leave Daddy. He was very weak, and because of his breathing problems I was terrified that he would die while I wasn't with him. Later, I heard him shuffling along the floor downstairs, and I was so glad that he was still alive.

I've been back from Granny's for what seems like ages, and the weather is getting colder. This morning, it's chilly, and I pull the covers up over my neck, even though I hate the weight of all the blankets on the bed, which feels like another body on top of me. I nestle my head on to Panda's leg, and my brain starts to think. Panda's my old pal. I got him the Christmas before last, when I was seven. Last Christmas, Santa didn't come. This had never happened before. All I know is that Mammy and Daddy were very drunk, maybe that had something to do with it, but my sister Clare got a tea chest, filled it with straw and put lots of little toys and sweets from Lucky Bags into it. It was actually one of the best gifts I ever got. I'll never forget sifting through the straw to see what I could find: it was so exciting. The previous Christmas Eve, though, I had seen my brother-in-law handing a big cuddly-toy panda down to Mammy from the attic. That was the end of that fantasy. But I do adore Panda. I chat away to him and tell him all my little worries from time to time.

I listen for any noise that might tell me whether Mammy's around. The radio volume seems a little lower than usual, and the house seems very still. I look out the window to see that Daddy's van has gone and I think, *Please God, let Mammy be gone out, too!* As I run downstairs, I realise that no one is at home and I begin to relax. I grab a handful of cornflakes for breakfast. It's eleven o'clock on a Sunday morning. I slept in late, but then I didn't go to bed till very late, because I was up watching *Hammer House of Horror* – and then I couldn't sleep. That's probably not surprising, because it's really scary. Nobody puts me to bed, so I just go up to bed when I feel sleepy.

I'd say they're gone to Molly's pub for a singsong. I settle in to do a bit of drawing, lay some paper on the front-room floor and start to draw the sun. It's always the first thing I draw on a picture, because it's my favourite thing. I am completely engrossed in my little world, until the next thing I know, I hear the van pulling up in front of the gate.

Oh, no. I must have been drawing for ages, and I can't believe it's the afternoon already. I need to be fast. Quick!

Quick! Quick! If she sees my drawings on the floor, she'll kill me. I never do any drawings in front of her because she'll just slag me off and say horrible things about them. I leg it upstairs just in time.

When they come in, the atmosphere has a thunderous tension to it. I decide that I'll wait up here till the coast is clear and then sneak out. The radio is switched on and is now blaring. I'd love to smash that and every other radio in this house, because the constant noise drives me mad. It's also a sign that things are about to take a turn for the worse. I take a chance and ease my way down the stairs. I look through the crack in the kitchen door and see Daddy sitting down at the table with his back to Mammy, who is at the cooker. His eyes are heavy with drink. She's uncomfortably quiet, and I'm just waiting for her next move. I've known this woman a few small years now, but she's always so unpredictable. Her actions always shock me, and then she shocks me some more.

Now she's slopping what looks like some part of an animal's head on to a plate. I can see that it's a cow's tongue. Oh, my God, I feel sick. She's slapping the plate with each aggressive scoop: potatoes, onions, parsnips. I'm not sure, but I swear I can see a smile on her face as she does so. I never see a smile on her face: is it possible that she's happy about something? The atmosphere tells me otherwise, and I always go with my gut. Suddenly, she swings around to face Daddy, slides his dinner along the table, juice spilling all over the surface, grabs the back of his head and, before I can even react, pushes his face with force into his dinner. 'Enjoy that!' she snaps.

Daddy is so drunk, he can only manage to turn his head to the side so he can breathe. The indignity of it. I feel paralysed, rooted to the spot. If she sees me now, I'm dead, because I couldn't move out of her way quickly enough if she caught me.

I gather myself and quietly go back up to Panda. Lying here, I'm thinking about how there's no other way out. Sometimes I wonder whether it would be easier for me not to be here any more. Would it be easier to just die? I can't imagine getting older, even though I feel a lot older than I am. I feel responsible for Daddy when he's drunk, and for Mammy when she's passed out on the couch. I keep checking that the oven, frying pans and other dangers are switched off, which they're often not. Sean and Clare, my brother and sister, don't stay around the house much, and I don't blame them. When I'm old enough, I'll be doing the exact same thing. When they are in the house, they let me hang around with them, and they stand up for me by telling Mammy to leave me alone when she screams at me in front of them, but they don't know what goes on when they're not here. Oh, to close my eyes at night and not be taut with tension would be a dream.

But whenever I think like this, something pulls me back, a curiosity about what might lie ahead for me in my own life, when I get out of here. I often wonder what I might be one day, when I'm older.

Talking of checking, I need to go downstairs and see if Daddy's alright. There's a lot of banging in the kitchen, but no shouting, and I'm not sure what that means. I sneak along the landing. Now I need to navigate some of the stairs. I'm only a scrap of a thing, so there isn't much body weight going on them, but still and all, the second I hear a creak on contact, I pull my toes straight back up and wait another couple of seconds. I make it halfway down the stairs and see Daddy in the front room. He's conked out by the writing desk and has his head bent at a dangerous angle. I hate when he sleeps like that: I'm always afraid he'll choke because of his breathing problems. He nearly drowned in the bath a couple of times when he fell asleep in the water. I need to straighten him up, but I also need to get in and out as quickly as I can. If I get my timing wrong, she'll swing her fist at me, and this always lands right by my ear.

Go! I dart over to him, gently lift his head, which is heavy, and tilt it to the side. I love this man and I don't want him to go yet, even though my gut is telling me it won't be long.

CHAPTER SIX

DRESSING UP

A FEW DAYS LATER, I gently go up the stairs, alert, as usual, for any sign of Mammy. As I pass the box room, which is now Daddy's bedroom, I see Daddy perched on the edge of the bed, watching the cars go by through the window. He often does that these days. He's always so quiet. Sometimes it drives me mad that he doesn't stand up for himself more. I think he's just been beaten down by Mammy. Daddy's only in his very early 50s, but he looks like an old man. He's so slow when he walks and can only take a few steps before he has to stop and catch his breath. The skin on the back of his neck is so wrinkled, and he smokes Sweet Afton cigarettes, one after the other. He never complains about his shortness of breath, and I don't understand why. I do get impatient with him sometimes, and I say, 'Come on, Daddy, will you hurry up?' He's often short-tempered these days and sounds cross a lot of the time, but he has never hit me and looks at me with his intense gaze. I could spend all day, every day with him. I trust this man with my life. I just wish sometimes that he could protect me from Mammy. Instead, I feel responsible for him whenever she attacks him, which is often. I think when they were going out together, Daddy might have loved Mammy more than she loved him. I can't explain it – it's just a feeling I have.

I do know that Daddy wasn't always like this, though. He used to be young and handsome, the son of an affluent family who live on the other side of the city. He's told me that when he married Mammy, they lived with his family in a huge house, and when they bought this house, it felt tiny. We don't see them any more, and I'm not really sure why.

Daddy often tells me that he used to love going to dances with Mammy when they first met, and now I like nothing more than to play dress-up with their old clothes, which they keep stored in the back bedroom. I catch a glimpse of what looks like a tailcoat. No way! I get excited, gently ease it off the hanger and try it on. I look at myself in the mirror. The tails are trailing on the floor, but I roll up the sleeves and immediately I transport myself into another world. Daddy was a bit of a dandy in his day and loved his tails, silk scarves and spats – I've seen him in photos, wearing his tails. He looked just like a handsome prince. Even now, he spends more time in the bathroom than anyone else. These days, he wears cardigans with leather patches on the elbows, slacks and Chelsea boots with steel caps on the heels. I love the sound they make. When I'm big, I'm going to wear Chelsea boots.

Mammy's old vinyl records are in a corner of this room as well. I notice that one of the covers has a picture of a ball on the front, with handsome men in tails and women in all their finery. I decide to put the record on the record player, lifting the needle carefully and placing it down on the black vinyl. Oh, God, the music is beautiful. Later that evening, I ask Daddy what that music is and discover it's Johann Strauss. Now I close the bedroom door tight and imagine that I'm one of those people on the album cover. I have an imaginary partner, and we waltz until we're dizzy. *Oh, that was brilliant*, I say to myself when the music stops.

I spend an awful lot of time in these fantasy worlds. The beauty about them is that I can direct them in whatever way I want. Another little thing that I can control. I love playing cowboy. I always play a hero cowboy, not a baddie, but one who seeks justice. But I'm certainly not afraid to swivel that gun in my hand and take a shot if I have to. The back dining room is where I play this one out. I imagine I'm in a saloon. I take down a little sherry glass and fill it with lemonade, swig it back and start chatting with my imaginary enemy. I could get a whole evening out of this one.

Another persona I have is that of detective. For this, I have a suit jacket borrowed from Daddy, a plastic brief-case full of dodgy fake money, a gun and a home-made ID, crafted out of a bit of scrap paper. I have a thing about IDs, I don't know what it is. Maybe it's the whole idea of putting your stamp on the world, a 'here I am, I exist' kind of thing. To me, there's nothing better than putting on fake plastic glasses and a fake moustache, and carrying a toy walkie-talkie in my hand. I feel big and powerful, like a proper grown-up.

Of all the roles I play, though, Dracula has to be my favourite. Mammy has a red wool cloak with navy silk lining that I turn inside out and wear when she's not around to see me. It's just perfect. To complete the look, I wear my school shirt with a dicky bow, black trousers, a waistcoat, white gloves, plastic fangs and my hair slicked back with Daddy's Brylcreem. Sometimes, I get a vial of fake blood from the joke shop: there's a great one on O'Connell Street, above a record store. The vial is a little breakable capsule that you crack with your teeth and feel the red liquid running down the corners of your mouth. It's just deadly. I usually play these games on my own at night when there's no one home.

Sometimes I get a bit obsessed with death. I don't know anyone who has died yet, but I'm terrified that one day Mammy is going to kill me or Daddy, and I don't want it to be painful. I always pray that if it's going to be me, please let it be quick. At other times, I kind of look forward to death, maybe because that way there will be no more threats, no more beatings. Mammy can't beat me if I'm dead.

I like to look after my clothes, even my school uniform, which I fold neatly at the end of the bed when I come home from school. I can't stand crumpled clothes, but it's hard to keep them looking nice when I'm such a tomboy. After a school day, I may end up with my socks around my ankles, my pockets turned out, my shirt tails out, my sleeves rolled up, my school tie loosened and my top buttons open, but I always have to start the day looking neat. It doesn't make sense to me, but later on maybe it will. It's the same when I'm not in school, which is a lot of the time. I have to start out looking smart, even if it all falls apart later in the day.

My blue shoes are the exception. They are navy lace-ups made of leather, but they are very scuffed at the toes because of all the climbing I do. It's almost like I'm grounding myself with them: they are my coat of armour, so to speak. They were too big when I got them and they're kind of tight on me by now, even though I haven't grown a whole lot. I wear them everywhere and every day. Sometimes I wear a tracksuit, but even then, I prefer to wear these shoes with it, rather than runners.

My shoes make me who I am. I feel stronger wearing them.

When my sister Maria got married, there was murder trying to get me into a bridesmaid's dress. Eventually I wore it, but only if I could wear my blue shoes with it. I'm a stubborn little kid. I'm never cheeky or answer back, but I'm determined. That's probably why I've survived this far. Anyway, the dress was full length, so the shoes were out of sight. I enjoyed that day, I have to say. I did miss the dessert, though, and there was a search party out for me. I don't know why: no one usually looks for me when I'm missing. Anyway, I was downstairs in the reception area, having the craic with a rugby team I'd met there. I was right in the middle of them, like I was in a scrum. I couldn't even be seen because I was so small in among the whole lot of them. It was a good laugh. I was brought back up to join the wedding and sneaked a bit of someone else's dessert.

CHAPTER SEVEN

WHAT NOBODY SEES

'M NINE NOW AND IN THIRD CLASS IN PRIMARY SCHOOL. Sometimes it can be hard going into the classroom for the day to learn things, when I've been awake half the night listening to Mammy and Daddy fight.

One evening, Daddy is slumped into his usual chair. He's sleepy. All is quiet, but as I head for the stairs and the safety of my bedroom, I hear Mammy coming out of the back dining room. For a moment, I can't believe what I'm seeing. She's wielding the green marble ashtray. This thing is so heavy, I can hardly lift it with two hands. She swings her arm back and screams, 'You bastard,' and launches the ashtray in Daddy's direction. It's as if it's happening in slow motion. My mouth opens, but nothing comes out. As the ashtray lands on Daddy's head, blood sprays on the wall like a fan.

I run to a neighbour, ready to say, 'Daddy's dead,' but even though I knock frantically, there's no one in. When I come back into the house, Daddy is on his knees in the front room, holding his head in his hands. Mammy is standing at the door. I get a tea towel and push past her to place it gently on his head. She laughs and says, 'Well, what do you think of your father now?'

Why is God doing this? I think, dabbing Daddy's wound. When will it end? Mammy's outbursts come out of nowhere. Sometimes I think that if I could just see inside her head, I'd know what she was thinking and be ready for it, but I can't. This time, neither of them is even drunk, but she still gets angry for no reason.

After what seems like ages, Mammy goes upstairs, and soon I can hear her radio in the bedroom, playing full blast. I sit quietly with Daddy and help him lie on the couch, which he does with a low moan. That night, I sneak down regularly to make sure he's still alive.

Now it's morning, and I need to get ready for school, even though I'm knackered. I check on Daddy. He's asleep and breathing. I breathe a sigh of relief. I get myself ready for school, but as I'm going out the back door, Mammy appears behind me. She can do that: creep up on you without a sound. 'Where the fuck do you think you're going?' she says and pulls me into the front room. She grabs the side of my head and scrapes it along the bloodied wall, the iron smell of Daddy's blood filling my nostrils. I feel sick. She then gets a bucket of water and a cloth and orders me to wash the blood off the wall before I go to school. I don't respond either way, because I know better than to say anything. I wring out the cloth and start wiping. Some of the blood gets on the cuff of my school shirt. When the task is over, I drop the cloth in the red water, kiss Daddy on the cheek and go out the back door and over the back wall to the lane that leads to the school. I feel like she has sucked the very soul out of me.

I come in late, and the teacher glances at me with expectation. I don't even try to come up with an excuse because I feel so tired. I just go straight to my desk. I'm barely settled when the bell goes for the small break. As we're heading out to the yard, the girls in front of me are talking about *Smash Hits* magazine and who was on *Top of the Pops*. I feel faint with exhaustion, and while wiping my nose on my cuff, I notice Daddy's blood again. I pull my sleeve over it and pray he's still alive.

After break, I'm sitting at my desk at the back of the class, beside the window, looking out at the side of the girls' school. There are separate buildings for boys and girls, but for some reason, we have to be in the boys' school for a while. It doesn't bother me at all, as I'm well used to the lads. I'm not sure what the teacher is talking about, though. I don't seem to be able to take anything in. If I do, I can't seem to hold on to it. I think that it's because I'm on constant high alert. I always feel anxious and ready to duck a blow. However, even though I don't understand a lot of what goes on here, school is a sanctuary, a refuge, a place where things happen when they're supposed to.

There's a knock on the door. The principal walks in and announces to the teacher that the nurse is here today, and we all have to go over to the girls' school in small groups to be 'assessed', whatever that means. After a while, my name, among others, is called out and we make our way over to the office in the girls' school. We sit on small chairs in the corridor and wait. Eventually, the nurse calls me in. She asks me my name and address. I know my name, but I couldn't tell you my address. She seems very surprised by this. I don't know why – it seems quite normal to me. Anyway, I never use the front door at home: I always come in through the back lane. That way, there's a better chance that *she* won't see me.

Questions over with, the nurse weighs me and says I'm 'a bit thin'. She then measures my height and checks my hair. 'Can you show me your fingernails?' she says gently.

I uncurl my fingers, as I usually have them closed to protect them. The spot underneath both thumbnails is infected with green pus, while on the other fingers, the cuticles are torn and bloodied, and the nails are bitten to nothing.

The nurse seems taken aback. 'Why do you bite your nails like that?' She looks at me carefully, her eyes searching mine.

Oh, my God, I think, *this is my chance. Please, please ask me more about it, and I'll tell you.* I'm dying to tell her everything, but all that comes out of my mouth is, 'Ah, it's me nerves.'

She pauses for a second before shaking her head and making a note in the register. I wait for her to say something, but she doesn't. I feel dejected. I wouldn't betray Mammy and Daddy voluntarily, but if I was asked, I would tell the honest truth about what goes on at home. Now I am so, so close to telling the nurse, but the words just won't come out. I can see the marble ashtray flying through the air, the blood spraying the walls, but I say nothing.

I'm back in the classroom, and we're doing religion now. I like the subject, because we always do lots of drawings in our copybooks, and I always put in the sun, the mountains, birds and trees around the religious figures. My teacher always says lovely things about my drawings, which makes me feel really good. Even though I feel so tired from this morning, drawing takes me away to a different place, and soon I'm colouring in a bright yellow sun and vivid green leaves on a tree, my feelings beginning to settle.

I rarely bring lunch to school with me, so at big break, I leg it straight to the girls' school and hope I make it in time to grab the lunch that is delivered every day. I like to grab a bottle of milk, which is always warm, but I don't mind. I love the cream on the top of it. Sometimes the birds will have already pecked through the tinfoil lid of the bottle, but that's alright; they need to survive as well. *Deadly*, I think, when I spot the delivery outside the school office; not only will I manage to get some milk, but also a hot-cross bun, even though I hate raisins. I also get a cheese sandwich. I'm pleased about this because some days it's corned beef sandwiches, which I can't stand. The margarine is thicker than the meat, and I try to swallow big chunks without chewing so I don't have to taste the beef, which is horrible. I now have a full belly. Today is looking up, even after a horrible start.

When I get home, I sneak in the back door, praying that Mammy isn't around. Then I smell the gas. One of them always leaves it on, and this terrifies me, because I imagine the house blowing up one day. I turn the oven off and sit down at the kitchen table. I try to make sense of the homework, but it's as if it has been written in a foreign language. I find homework really hard, because I don't go to school often enough to understand everything, and a lot of the time there's no one to help me at home. My sister Clare does help me when she can, but she's with her friends a lot of the time or has her own homework to do. Sean is out working and doing his own thing, and Mammy never helps me. Sometimes when I'm desperate, I do ask her, but she just tells me to fuck off. Maybe it's because she's so tired after working all day. I wouldn't even ask Daddy because he's always exhausted.

After a while, I give up, grab a slice of bread and head out the back. Eventually, when the sun sets and I've witnessed every last bit of light dip into the earth, I head back into the house. I creep upstairs and slide into bed. I lie there on Panda, thinking about ashtrays that fly through the air and wiping blood off the walls and why I didn't tell the nurse, even though I was bursting to. Maybe I was too scared of what might happen if I did. Maybe I thought that they'd take me away, and I'd never see Mammy and Daddy again. I know that I hate what goes on sometimes, but I don't want that. I'd miss my brothers and sisters and Panda and Dave and Ger and the cornfield. As my eyelids droop, I see myself running through Murph's golden field, free as a bird. Soon, I'm fast asleep.

CHAPTER EIGHT

AN ADVENTURE WITH DADDY

A FEW WEEKS AFTER THE NURSE'S VISIT, I'm lying in bed, dreading the day ahead. The teacher said the bishop was coming in today. I only found out yesterday, because I wasn't in school for a few days. We all have to know our catechism, and teacher said that the bishop will be very disappointed if we don't. I don't really know what the catechism is. I think it might be a kind of rule book, but I never learned it, so I'm not going to be put in that trap, no matter who he is.

Daddy knows nothing about the bishop coming in, but now that Mammy has gone to work for the day, I can beg him to keep me off school. Daddy always lets me stay home. He doesn't take much convincing, and he simply says, 'Okay, Tiger.' Then he warns me not to say anything to Mammy, because she'll kill him. It'll be our secret.

Daddy tells me he has to do a bit of work in the cash and carry and asks if I want to go along with him. I nearly wet myself with excitement. We get into the van, and I get my big elastic band from the glove compartment, wrap one part of the band around the door of the compartment, then close it. The piece that's exposed is now my horse's rein. I sit right on the front edge of the seat, so I can see as much as possible out the window. Every single pothole and bounce the van makes gives me joy, as I imagine I'm galloping on a horse.

For my ninth birthday, Daddy brought me to some riding stables and let me go on a horse. It was deadly, and I'm dying to go again. 'Come on, giddy-up, pony!' I say over and over as I bounce on the front seat with my daddy beside me. I couldn't be happier.

Daddy's job is to do deliveries, and after dropping something off at the cash and carry, he needs to deliver something to Woolworths. I love this shop, it's huge! You could spend all day in here. The real reason I'm attracted to it is because of the colours. I've never seen anything like them in my life. At the front of the shop, there's a massive row of see-through cabinets with bursts of colour inside. On closer inspection, I can't believe my eyes: it's sweets! How can there be so many different types? I see gobstoppers, fizzle sticks, liquorice pipes and loads more. I'm just standing there, staring at the rainbow colours in front of me. They remind me of the bright colours I use in my drawings. After a few minutes, I slowly raise my hand to the cabinet with the bull's eyes in it. I open the door, take one out and flick it into my mouth. Oh, yeah. When the coast is clear, I stick another few sweets in my trouser pockets and innocently walk away.

Just then I hear: 'Tiger!' It's Daddy. He hasn't spotted me taking the sweets, thank God. He takes my hand, and as we go out, we pass a photo booth. I'm trying to figure it out, then Daddy explains it to me in more detail: the way you can close the curtain, sit on the seat in front of the screen and wait for the camera inside it to flash, taking a tiny photo of you. I beg him to bring me in and show me how it works. He gives in eventually, and we sit in, pulling the curtain closed. Daddy swivels the seat as high as it will go, sits me on it then pops in some money. I have a 10-pence piece in my pocket, and I add that to his change.

The camera flashes once, twice, three, four times. I'm wearing my navy nylon shirt, buttoned up to the neck, and a navy double-breasted blazer with a crest on it. I feel like some kind of captain when I'm wearing this. As I see the photos emerging slowly from inside the booth, it feels like a magic trick. I'm going to keep this photo safe, and I'll remember this day forever.

We get back home before Mammy, and she has no idea what we were up to. If she knew Daddy kept me off school, he'd probably be in big trouble. It would just be an excuse to cause a fight.

A few days later, I'm in school when the bell goes at the end of the day. I take my time packing up. I'm always the last one to leave the room, because I don't really want to go home. This time, as I pass the wooden prefab, I get the usual whiff of creosote. It's the brown smelly stuff that's painted on the wood to stop it rotting. Ugh, I hate that smell. I look straight ahead and see a familiar figure in the distance. *That's Daddy, what's he doing here?* I think. He never collects me. I know it's him for sure, because he's slow and hunched, his shoulders pushed right up around his neck. I kind of feel embarrassed, and then I feel bad that I do because I love my daddy to bits.

As I look around at the other parents collecting their kids, it strikes me for the first time how young and energetic they all seem. I see a daddy lift his child up and put him on his shoulders effortlessly. Another girl runs to her daddy, then he, in turn, chases her as they laugh. A boy kicks a ball to his dad, and the dad then tackles the boy playfully. The mammies don't seem as playful, but they smile and gently hold their kids' hands. Some mammies even hug their kids. Wow. I often wonder what it would feel like to have Mammy touch me gently, but I very quickly dismiss the idea, because I know it's a stupid one.

As Daddy gets closer, I can hear the ferocious wheeze in his chest. When he gets to me, he can't talk. He has to stop, cough and try to catch his breath. Again, I feel embarrassed, and even annoyed. I'm thinking in my head that this man should be walking tall and briskly. Instead, he looks small and pathetic. He looks so old and weak in himself. I quickly feel sad and sorry for him. I so wish we could run around and have more fun together. I wouldn't expect him to climb trees with me or get on top of the coal shed or watch one of my avalanches, but it would be lovely to kick a ball around with him in the park, or even in the garden. He's never in the garden: he's either driving the van, sitting on his bed, staring out the window or slumped in the chair in the front room. Sometimes, when he's in his chair and the wheeze isn't so bad, I'll ask him to draw me a horse. He's brilliant at art and particularly at drawing horses. Some day I hope I can draw horses like he can.

It turns out that Daddy has collected me because we are having a haircut this afternoon. Brilliant. I can't wait. My hair is parted at the side and cut short in a boy's style. I like it this way, because it doesn't bother me when I'm climbing or messing about. People often think that I'm a boy. I don't think I mind being mistaken for a boy – sometimes I feel like one myself. I look like one, and I love getting into scrapes and mischief, just like the boys in my neighbourhood. I particularly like playing with boys' toys. Sometimes, I wonder if I like it because I feel stronger that way, as if I'm the man of the house, not Daddy. I just don't feel like a girl.

Daddy wears his hair slicked straight back. His hair is really thin nowadays, not like when he was younger, but the way Daddy looks now is the only way I've ever known him. We head off down the road to the barber's shop, which is quite close. I hold Daddy's hand and, as we walk slowly, always slowly, I hear the click of his shoes. Now that's a sound I love. I feel a comfort when I'm with him and it's just the two of us. Daddy never has a whole lot to say. I think it's because he's always tired, but he's so affectionate and gentle. He always smiles at me and holds my hand. I don't even have to ask him.

We get to the barber's shop, and the excitement is rising up inside me. I love this experience. I feel like such a grown-up when I'm here, chatting away with all the men. I can be very quiet and thoughtful at times, and at others, I just open my mouth and it falls out. The barber gets the plank of wood he keeps specially for children and places it across the armrests of the seat. The man then lifts me on top of it. Daddy's not able to lift me at the moment, but that's okay. Wow! I'm now the same height as Daddy, who's in the chair beside me. I'm on top of the world.

I generally prefer looking like a boy, but it does get a little awkward at times. I was in town with Mammy one day in one of the big department stores, and she went to use the toilet. I didn't need to go, so I waited outside. She seemed to be taking ages. I was starting to get restless. I'm like that: I can never seem to relax and switch off. I always have to keep going. Anyway, eventually, I walked over to the main door of the ladies' toilets and peeked in. I couldn't see her. I started pacing up and down and noticed a security guard coming slowly in my direction. I could swear he was looking at me. I wasn't stashing anything in my pockets that day, so it wasn't that.

I went to take one more look inside the ladies' toilets, and the next thing I knew, I was grabbed by the collar of my top. As I swung around, I saw the security man looming over me. 'Get out of here, you little pervert!'

I was confused. I explained that I was just waiting on my mammy. He ordered me to wait a good distance from the ladies' toilets. He pointed his finger at me as he marched away. It was only then that I copped on. He thought I was a boy!

I listen to the chat between the barber and Daddy as he has his thin hair trimmed, and then it's my turn. The scissors hover over my head, *snip, snip*, and the barber pushes the comb through my hair. As I look in the mirror, I smile, because I see myself turning back into a boy. *That's better*, I think.

A few days later, I'm sitting with Mammy and Daddy in their usual spot in the local pub. Every weekend, they spend all day in the pub, drinking and singing. I try and leg it out of the house before they go, so I'm not dragged along with them. Today I wasn't quick enough, though. Thankfully, I have my Matchbox battleship that Daddy brought home for me last Sunday after the pub. The ship is deadly! It's about six inches long and very narrow. The hull itself is metal, and the plastic guns on the top can spin around. I never seem to run out of different scenarios for my new toy – there's always an enemy: that's the common theme. I see the girls in school playing nice, happy games with their dolls, who all seem to have plenty of doll friends. My games are about the survival of the fittest – may the best man win. I can't afford to show weakness to the enemy.

Mammy and Daddy are sitting with a group of people at the bar. I have no idea who they are; I was just told to stay out of their way. I am exploring around in the background. Daddy then shifts in his seat and goes to stand up. I always seem to have one eye on him, and when I see him get up, I ask, 'Where are you going, Daddy?'

'To the toilet,' he says.

'Here,' I say, 'wait for me. I want to go for a slash as well.' With that, I leave my battleship to fight its own battle for a while and head to the jacks with Daddy. Now I am just like one of the other lads. As I saunter in behind Daddy, the first thing that hits me is the smell. Wow, that's a new experience! It reminds me of the toilets in the boys' school, but it's a lot worse. There are these big balls of disinfectant all over the urinals. I don't know which smells worse, the urine or the disinfectant. Both sting the nostrils out of me.

I stand at the urinal along with Daddy and the other men. There is an almost military feel to it, something very ordered. I like that. I watch as all the streams meet together and then join in unison along the bottom gully, flowing right along and eventually down the drain in the corner. No one pays any heed to the fact that I am there. Sure, I keep forgetting, that's probably because they think I am a boy. *Well, at least no one is going to kick me out of the gents for being a pervert!* I laugh to myself. Job done, most of the men zip up, nod to each other and walk out. No hanging around, no gawking in mirrors or yakking away for ages, like they seem to do in the ladies' toilet. I am kind of bursting to go myself now. I ask Daddy to wait while I head into one of the cubicles. When I'm finished, I run a bit of water over my hands in the sink and rub my hands on my trousers to dry them off. 'That was fab,' I say. I'd never been in the gents before. Now it's back to the open seas with my battleship.

CHAPTER NINE

SINK OR SWIM

MY DADDY IS MY FAVOURITE PERSON IN THE WORLD, even if he doesn't offer me much protection from Mammy – I know that it's because he's not strong enough. Every day, he seems to get a little weaker. His cough has grown worse over the past year, and when he walks he's hunched over even more than before. I'm only nine years old, but even so, my gut tells me that he won't be here for me much longer. He's taken to walking to the big church up the road every day, and I'm not sure why. Maybe he's saying his prayers, hoping that God will let him into heaven.

Now it's a Saturday afternoon, and Daddy is fast asleep in the front room, as usual. He seems to do that more and more these days. When I hear a knock on the front door, I answer it. Standing on the doorstep is Matt, a friend of my brother Sean. He's dead on – it's like having another big brother. When he asks me if I want to go swimming in the local pool, I think, *Is he joking?* I can't believe somebody could be so thoughtful. Damn right I want to go!

I fly upstairs, grab my togs, goggles and a towel, and head off with Matt. I'm now feeling awkward because I have no money. By my expression, Matt guesses what the problem is. 'It's okay, I'll treat you today,' he says. We walk in silence for a bit, then Matt says, 'I can call in for you whenever I go swimming, if you like.' I'd love that, and my swimming will get better, I know, with a bit of practice. I haven't had any lessons. I'm not bothered about why Matt is asking me. I wonder briefly if Sean has something to do with it, but I don't care. I'm just so happy to be somewhere else, away from that house.

I love everything about the pool. I love that echoey sound the minute you step inside the front door, the blast of humid air and the sheer anticipation of getting into the water. The pool was one of the few things that I did like about Butlin's on our holiday there. I used to love going down under the water, my goggles over my eyes, and being able to see the people on the footpath outside through the glass wall under the pool. I also used to be fascinated by the various shapes and sizes of all the arms and legs belonging to the people splashing about in the water.

I realise now that I've forgotten my inflatable armbands. I like to have them on as extra security, because I'm not that confident a swimmer yet. I decide that I'm quite happy just to float around the baby pool. Matt says he's going to the deep end and to give him a shout if I need him. As I step in, I see the baby pool is fairly quiet today. I'm delighted to have all this space to myself and I can splash about at my leisure. After a while, I hop up on to the pool's edge and watch all the others in the big pool. I start to daydream. This is also a favourite activity of mine. I daydream quite a lot, disappearing into imaginary worlds, far away from the one I live in.

I start to think about the day I learned to swim. It wasn't something I'd planned, and it certainly wasn't what I'd expected. I was about seven years old, and we went on a picnic, just Daddy, Mammy, Enda and me. Even though Enda is my older brother, we don't talk much. I never see Mammy pick on Enda, because I think she's afraid of him. Enda throws things and has a temper: he can't help it, though, because he gets frustrated. His words get jumbled up, and lots of people don't know what he's saying. I can understand him, though.

I was dreading the picnic, because I knew that it would begin with big flasks of tea, sandwiches and bottles of Guinness, but it would probably end in a horrible fight. I've no idea where we went, only that when we eventually got to this big field, I couldn't really relax as I was dreading the journey home already, with Daddy and Mammy screaming at each other and the van weaving all over the road.

This time, it didn't begin too badly. Daddy told me to go and climb a tree, which I did, taking Enda with me, climbing high up above the field, looking down at Mammy and Daddy sitting on the picnic rug, drinking and smoking. It felt good to be up there, far away from them. I felt safe in my canopy with Enda.

Sometime later, I saw Daddy come towards the tree with an empty bottle crate and a rope in his hand. *What's he up to?* I wondered. He then threw the rope over a large branch, turned the crate upside down and attached one end of the rope to each side of the crate. I couldn't believe he was just after making a swing for us! I was beside myself with excitement. Enda laughed and clapped his hands. That was us occupied for the afternoon.

Later, with everything packed up, we headed off again. Now, we were driving along the seafront. Daddy pulled in and parked. Mammy turned to tell me that my swimming togs were in the back of the van if I wanted to get changed and head for the water with Daddy. She would stay in the van with Enda and watch us both. Oh, that was brilliant!

I climbed into my togs in no time at all, and I hopped out of the van. Daddy stripped off, and for the first time I really noticed his bare chest. Daddy has a big barrel chest. I think what makes it look bigger is that his shoulders seem always to be pushed up these days. It's from trying to catch his breath as much as he can. For some reason it reminds me of the turkey under Mammy's arms that Christmas.

I loved the feeling of the air on my bare skin. It felt so freeing. Daddy took my hand, and we walked towards the water. I couldn't wait to run up and down the shore, kicking the water with my feet, but before I knew it, Daddy grabbed me by the waist and tucked me under his arm. I just laughed because I loved a bit of horseplay. We walked closer and closer to the water. When we got to the froth at the edge of the water, I prepared for him to put me on my feet at any second, but no, he kept going.

I was getting uneasy now. When we got to the point where the water was up to his knees, I started to panic a little. Then I remembered that this was my daddy and he never purposely put me in danger, but as I looked down, the ocean was slowly making its way up to my face. The water was now at Daddy's waist. Then I felt myself falling into the water. I started screaming with panic, flailing my arms about, my mouth filling with water. I couldn't believe it: Daddy had just dropped me in. I yelled for him, but not once did he turn around, laughing as he walked out of the water. I could see other people in the distance, but my cry was going unheard. The reality hit me that I could either manage to get out or drown. I swung my arms and legs with all my might and somehow

I managed to stay above the water while moving towards the shore. I kept up this frantic movement for as long as it took until, eventually, I crawled the last bit. I collapsed on the sand, tears streaming down my face. I'd never felt terror at Daddy's hands until now.

Daddy walked up to me and said, 'Well done, now you can swim.' How did he know I was going to survive it? That was the one thing about Daddy: physically he was no match for Mammy, but at the same time, he didn't have any fear. He took chances, and he also had no sense sometimes, doing things without thinking about what might happen next. It was an experience I will never forget. It did work, though. I learned to swim, because otherwise, I'd have drowned. Soon, I found myself able to leave my armbands at home when I went to the swimming pool.

CHAPTER TEN

MY FRIENDS, THE STONES

T'S NOW SPRING 1980. I'll be ten in July. I am climbing the swing out in the back garden, pretending it's a ship and I am the captain. 'Ahoy, me maties!' I say as I peer through the tube of the empty toilet roll that is serving as my telescope. You have to be careful of the enemies in the ocean. I get a piece of Daddy's blue rope from the shed, the same piece that Action Man is often dragged around with. I hurl it over the swing and pretend that I am adjusting my sails.

The next thing I hear a cry. 'Rasher!' That's my nickname. I don't know how I got it, but that's what a lot of the lads call me. I see that it's Shay, who lives down the road. He scales the wall after I greet him and joins my imaginary crew on the ship. There is a storm brewing, and we stand on the swing seat, swinging it forwards and backwards, holding on to the ropes tightly on each side.

It's good craic, but I am getting a little dizzy. That's the only thing about some of these adventures: it doesn't take much to make me dizzy these days. I think it's from Mammy hitting me on the side of the head. She does that a lot now, and it makes my head swim.

After another few minutes of the stormy seas, we suddenly call a halt and hop off. We plonk ourselves on the mucky ground and say nothing for a while. It's a really comfortable silence. I relish these moments. There are two types of silence in my life. The first is where I am listening out to suss the atmosphere, to judge if it's safe to walk out of my bedroom to the toilet or to go out through the kitchen to the back garden without getting a clatter to the side of the head. Sometimes, I am bursting to go to the toilet, but I'll still wait until I know the coast is clear. I'm often in pain by the time I actually get there.

The second silence is this kind of silence, a safe one, where I can be in someone's company and not feel under any kind of pressure to talk. I can simply relax and enjoy playing games and making up adventures.

Shay pipes up after a bit and suggests we go swimming. I nod and tell him to meet me outside the pool. With my togs, towel and goggles together, I am off. I don't need to wear my armbands any more, and I feel kind of proud of myself. It's like my first little milestone in life. I'm still a little wary of Daddy, though, after he threw me in the sea. I don't think he meant to be cruel, and I suppose it did teach me to swim.

I grab the money for the pool from my little piggy bank, and before I know it, Shay and I are in the shallow end of the pool and loving it. I'm pleased that I paid for my ticket myself. I don't get pocket money, but I sometimes get money from the jobs that I do every Friday for Mammy. Because she comes from a family of shopkeepers, she believes in hard work. Sometimes I have to do dusting, other times I use the Brasso polish to clean the ornaments on the hall table. The dusting is easy, but Mammy's inspections make my stomach ache, because I know what'll happen if the furniture isn't sparkling clean. She lifts up the rugs and looks at the bottom of the chair legs. If she sees a bit of dust, which she always does, she belts me across the head. I have to stand beside her while she's doing the inspections, and I swear she must plant some balls of dust while I am not looking, so she will have an excuse to hit me – not that she usually needs one. But it's hard to say no to the money, so it's a double-edged sword.

While we are splashing about, I can't help but gulp some water filled with chlorine, and my stomach begins to swell. Later, when we are dry and dressed, I meet Shay outside the back of the pool, and we decide to hang around in the playground for a bit. I love sitting on the wooden horse with the big spring underneath it, instead of legs. A sharp pain in my gut suddenly startles me. 'Ohh,' I moan. I get off my horse. I don't even remember saying goodbye to Shay, as I was so distracted. As I am walking towards the main road, I feel a warm, watery sensation in my underpants. I don't believe this. How am I going to make it from here to the house without it coming down the leg of my trousers? Not only that, but how am I going to clean these clothes so no one will ever know? If Mammy's at home, she will kill me. If it's Daddy, he just won't know what to do.

I have no choice but to go into the house. I scuttle up to the front door, because if I try and go over the back wall, it'll be everywhere. As I am walking up the stairs, now in tears, waiting to meet my fate, the diarrhoea is making its way to my shoes.

I meet Daddy at the top of the stairs. Ah, thank God! If it was Mammy, I'd be in big trouble. 'She's going to kill me,' I wail, as the tears fall. I just can't stop.

'It's okay, Tiger,' Daddy says. He takes my hand and leads me to the toilet. He tells me, reassuringly, to take everything off. I don't feel one bit embarrassed or awkward. I would if it was Mammy: I'd feel humiliated. The shoes, trousers, socks and underpants come off slowly. Daddy gets a cloth and cleans me up. As I get into clean clothes, he puts the soiled ones into a bucket and takes them downstairs. I don't know what he does with them after, but I do know she doesn't find out. I feel safe with that man. I go from feeling sheer terror to sheer relief when I know it's just him and me.

Later, Mammy comes home from work in a foul mood. I know that she works in a home for mothers and babies, and I wonder if she likes the little babies better than me. Maybe she liked me when I was a baby. Maybe she was very sad when Noelle died. Now, I stay well out of her way. I go into the front room and play with Action Man. Later, she bursts in through the door in a temper. She has a plate of food in her hand, and when I look at it, it makes my stomach churn. It still feels a bit sick after the chlorine, but I'm not about to tell Mammy that.

'Get into the kitchen and eat this,' she says.

'I'm not really hungry,' I say nervously. At first, she says nothing, just walks out of the room. I turn on the telly to see if there are any cartoons on. I love *Popeye*, and so does Daddy. I also love *Road Runner* and *The Pink Panther*. Now I discover that *Black Beauty* is on. Deadly – I love this show about a wild black horse and its adventures.

The next thing, there's another bang of the front-room door, and she's looming over me while I am on my hunkers in front of the telly. 'You'll eat when I fucking decide you'll eat!' She jabs at the TV set, on which an ad for the charity Trócaire is now showing. 'How would you like it if you were one of those children who had no choice but to be hungry?' she roars. Her nostrils are now flaring. She puts the palm of her hand on my cheek and presses my face against the TV screen. Then she gets a fork, scoops up whatever is on the plate – I don't even recognise it – and forces the fork through my lips. If I keep my mouth closed, the prongs will just stab me, so I have no choice but to open it. She pushes the food through violently, but I can't swallow as I keep gagging. As she is forcing it in, it keeps oozing back out in equal measure.

'Look at that poor starving child,' she says. 'May God forgive you, that's all I can say.' She now smears the food that is coming out of my mouth all over my face. With that, she straightens herself up and walks away.

I disappear into my other world for a bit and fantasise about being dead. If this is going to be my life, hopefully it won't be too much longer before it's over.

The next morning, I stick on my red Converse runners instead of my blue shoes for a change. When I finish getting dressed, I go straight out the back. I'm not even hungry this morning. I have a strange relationship with food. Nowadays Mammy makes me eat dinner, but otherwise it's not something I think about, and I only eat when my stomach starts to rumble. I scale the back wall and sit on the top for a while, listening to the birds. I could just look at the sky all day. I imagine faces in the clouds and God somewhere among them. I do believe in

God, but I also struggle to understand how cruel some people can be. Why would God make people like that? I edge my bum out as far as I can, so I'm ready to jump and land nimbly on my feet. 'Shit.' I'm after scraping the back of my thigh. I'm always doing that. I'm forever giving myself cuts and bruises. I don't mind the sight of blood at all. I think the weekend activities in the house make me immune to all that, and I seem to have a good pain threshold.

I remember playing 'rocks' with a neighbourhood kid once. He has a shed at both ends of his garden. We took up our positions in front of each shed, opened the shed doors and used them as shields while we flung stones at each other. He gave me a bloodied head one day. I was impressed with his aim. My aim wasn't bad either. His mammy was mortified and insisted I go in to my mammy to tell her that he'd hit me. I said that I was grand and that getting cut didn't bother me, but she wasn't having any of it. When I did go in to Mammy, she gave me a slap across the head for being so stupid. I went back, and we secretly resumed our game. It was great craic.

Now it's time for Action Man. I eye Mammy's vege-table plot and decide that it'll be the jungle and that he's just been captured and is awaiting his fate. I'll put him through some grisly torture. When Mammy's not at work or making dinner, she has a plot in the garden for growing fruit and vegetables. It's maybe 30 feet long and 20 feet wide, with rows of scallions and rhubarb and cabbage. She has it growing right up to the back of the house. I love the smell of the soil, especially when it's been turned over. But what I love most of all are my little friends, the caterpillars.

The back of the house is covered in pebbledash, but that doesn't stop my furry green friends crawling right up to the eaves. When I see caterpillars crawling on the footpath, I very quickly and gently pick them up and place them back in the soil, on familiar ground, away from danger. I really enjoy the sensation of them crawling along my hand and leaving a deposit of green, as they fold themselves along. Stroking their little furry bodies and chatting away to them passes many an hour.

As I place Action Man in his hiding place underneath a head of cabbage, I remember Paul, another neighbour, and how I scared him once with the caterpillars. He'd been following me around the garden like a puppy. I don't mind company, but when I want to be alone, I seriously want to be alone. Paul wasn't getting the message, and after loads of attempts to encourage him to do his own thing for a bit, I had an idea. I got a handful of caterpillars from their munching ground, very carefully closing my fingers around them, and went back down to Paul, who was now sitting with his back to me. I told him I wanted to show him something and to close his eyes. I brought my cupped hands up close to his face, opened up my fingers and told him he could now look.

Well, at the sight of the caterpillars crawling around on my hand, he jumped to his feet and squealed. I ran after him, yelling, 'But Paul, they're lovely!' He scaled the back wall to get away, and I stood there chuckling to myself, until I could hear his footsteps in the distance. I think he got the message. Very quickly, I walked back to the cabbage patch, knelt down carefully and tilted both hands right down to the soil, until each furry creature was back on its familiar ground.

Action Man has been captured by the enemy and tortured, and I'm getting bored with that game. I decide to move him to the back lane for some watery adventures. There's a part of the back laneway that's always full of water. I walk along the mucky verge when I'm coming along the lane. Whenever I see pebbles or stones that have fallen off the verge, I always feel compelled to pull them out with a stick and place them gently back on the edge again. It's as if these stones have a little life of their own, and I want to bring them to safety. I chat away to them and I imagine them responding, so we have imaginary two-way convers- ations. The little stones in the lane are too vulnerable. When I place them together, I always imagine that they're back with all their family and safe again.

CHAPTER ELEVEN

MAMMY'S GAMES

SOMETIMES, MAMMY ATTACKS ME SEVERAL TIMES A WEEK. It's not so much the physical beatings that I find hard – sometimes I can even zone out from the pain, though when she hits me on the side of my head with her fist, I always feel like I'm going to faint. This makes my eyesight blurry too, at times. It's more the psychological fear that makes me want to break in two when I do something wrong or when she wants to play one of her twisted games.

Her favourite at the moment is chasing me around the house with a butcher's knife in her hand. For me, the waiting for it to happen is worse than the attack itself. Take the night I decided to do a bit of art in the front room. Mammy was just after getting a new oatmeal-coloured carpet fitted in the front room, and I was warned not to play on it. Mammy is very house-proud and she's always buying new things for the house. She likes to put up new wallpaper and to keep it spick and span. A lot of the furniture in the house is very old and grand, because it came from Daddy's family home.

Daddy was in hospital with his breathing problems again, Mammy was gone to the pub, and I was alone in the house. I felt that I could breathe, for once, and I set up my blue ink brushes and paper on the desk in the front room. I missed Daddy, but I took comfort in the knowledge that he was safe there. I decided I'd paint him a picture in ink, because he really liked my pictures, and I set to work. Then I went to clean the brush in the water, and my arm made contact with the ink bottle, knocking it off the desktop straight on to the new carpet. It was one of those moments when I wished I was dead.

I got water in the kitchen and scrubbed and scrubbed and scrubbed at the stain, which only seemed to make it worse. The blue wasn't as dark as it had been, but it had spread to become a larger stain right in the middle of the carpet. Eventually, I gave up and resigned myself to the fact that I wasn't going to hide this one. I tidied everything else away and opened the front door to check if she was on her way. I wanted to tell her before she came in and saw it. I walked up and down the driveway and stood at the gate numerous times. After three hours of this pacing in the driveway, she walked in the gate. I stopped her in her tracks and told her exactly what had happened. She said nothing, just went into the front room to survey the damage. I stood outside, waiting, before creeping into the front room, where she was on her hands and knees, scrubbing.

I don't know how, but whatever she did, she managed to get most of it out. The one thing about Mammy is that she can do anything she puts her mind to, whether it's saving money or getting rid of stains.

As I watched her get rid of the ink stain, I felt so relieved that I thought she would maybe be a little lenient as a result. Instead, she walked slowly towards the front-room door and closed it gently, but firmly. She stared me right in the eye and pulled up her sleeves. This was to be the first of many times Mammy would hit me on the left side of my head, right on my ear. I can't describe the pain. It was like a burning, dizzying sensation, followed by a numbness in my ear. Sometimes, after one of Mammy's clatters to the head, I feel like I'm submerged under water, and there's also a horrible, high-pitched humming sound in my ear, like white noise, which makes me feel dizzy and nauseous. I wonder if she hits me there because no one will see the bruise under my hair? I wear it slightly longer at the sides at this point, and it's only when I lift it that you can see the big blue bruise, like the ink stain on the carpet.

When she'd finished with me, she grabbed me by the shoulders and shoved me against the wall. I stood there till she left and then just slid down to the floor.

*

The next time I get a beating is when I've been out play-ing for the afternoon. Before I go in the back door, I slap my knees to get as much dust off me as possible. The minute I open the door, I can smell the burn of alcohol in the air. When I get that smell, I know there'll be trouble.

I can't tell the time because I can't read the clock, even though I'm nine years old. I close that door so gently behind me that it hardly makes a sound, and I tiptoe to the other end of the kitchen. My indoor world is made up of little landmarks in each room: in the kitchen, if I get as far as the cooker, that's good; as far as the table, better again. If I reach the door leading into the hallway, I've almost made it to safety. Now the hallway can be tricky because I have to get past the two doors, to the back room and the front room, without being seen, before I can scuttle upstairs. I don't see anyone in either room. She must be upstairs, I figure, so I'll just stay down here.

As I pass the downstairs bedroom, which was con-verted from a garage when Daddy had to move into the other bedroom not long ago, because of his chest, the door suddenly swings wide open. Oh, Jesus! There she is, drunk, swaying in front of me. I'm stuck and can't move. This is what happens when she appears like this: it's as if she shocks me into place. She has that horrible contor-tion on her face that she gets when she's drunk, her lips twisted into a snarl. She says, 'Let's play a game of hide and seek.'

My heart starts to race. She never plays with me. What is she up to? She's now standing right in the middle of the hallway, blocking my way to the front door, the back door and any of the downstairs windows through which I might try to escape. She tells me my time starts now. She begins to count, 'One, two, three, four...'

I bound up the stairs and scan the rooms for a hiding place. Eventually, I crawl on to the top shelf of a cupboard on the landing. I can hear my heart thundering out of my chest, the tick-tock of the clock on the wall seeming to get louder and louder. I can hear my blood rushing, just like you can hear the ocean when you put one of those big sea-shells to your ear. That fast sea gushing its spray into the heavens, the seagulls gliding above in an atmosphere of complete serenity... it's all so different from this.

Tick-tock, tick-tock. *I'm going to die.* That's all that goes through my head. This is it. Will anyone ever find me? The teachers in school won't come looking for ages, because I'm hardly ever in. *Whatever it is, please God, make it be quick*, I think.

'Now let me see... where are you?' she says from outside.

I can't stand the suspense. I now hear a tapping sound, like an object being dragged along the banisters. I can't work out what it is at first, but it sounds as if it might be metal. It's getting louder and louder. The methodical sound is making its way closer to me. I curl up tightly in the cupboard. There's silence, then the door of my hiding place opens.

I see a glint of metal. I look up, and all I see is her face, looming over me. 'Look what I have,' she says, brandishing one of the butcher's knives from the kitchen.

Now I go to a different place and actually feel quite calm. It's as if someone has flicked a switch, and all my senses are suddenly turned off. I feel nothing.

She proceeds to press the tip of the knife under my chin and laughs as she says, 'I could kill you right now.'

I look her in the eye and tell her, 'Do it.'

'I can, you know, because you're simply nothing,' she replies.

My senses are floating back. Tears are now filling my eyes. I feel so much hatred for her at the moment that it's overwhelming. I now beg her to do it. Nothing could be worse than this. I can't go on like this any more. I'm now thinking, *What if I grabbed the top of my head and pushed it down on to the knife? Would that work? Would I be killed immediately? Because I need to know.*

The blade is still pressed to my chin, and I feel exhausted all of a sudden. I just want it to be over.

With that, she suddenly stands up and says, 'Don't you ever forget it.' She turns around and goes back down the stairs.

I eventually roll out of my tiny space and crawl on all fours to the bedroom, too weak with tension to stand on my feet. I crawl on to the bed clutching at Panda's legs. This is where I stay until the next sunrise.

CHAPTER TWELVE

ENTOMBED

I FEEL LONELY THESE DAYS. Daddy tells me he's sad the whole time and that he wants to die. He spends a lot of time in and out of the hospital with his chest and really struggles when he's walking now. A few times he's signed himself into the psychiatric hospital at Grange-gorman. Daddy told me it was to get away from Mammy for a break, but I know my daddy's going to die soon. I can't see my life without him. No more calling me 'Tiger', no more outings in his little van, with me on the front seat on my pony. No more hearing the click of his Chelsea boots as he walks up the front drive. I can't believe that he's going to leave me here with Mammy.

My sister Clare is still around at the moment, and when she's here, I feel that Mammy can't get to me. Last night, she even invited me into her bedroom to hang around with her friends. She had the fire on and incense burning, and it was really cosy. I felt safe and relaxed for the first time in months. But it won't be long now until it'll just be Mammy and me. The thought makes my heart flutter in panic.

One morning, I pull the blankets up under my chin and reach my toes around to find the hot-water jar. It's early summer, but it's cold. I love this jar, and I use it every night. It's really old. Mammy brought it up from the country when she first moved up to Dublin when she was about twenty, and when I use it, I wonder what she was like then. I wonder if she was happy when she was young. I know that she was clever, because once she told me that she won a scholarship to go to nursing college. I don't think she went, though. I wish I was as clever as her.

The hot-water jar is a long, brown ceramic jar with a screw cap on top, and it keeps the water hot for ages. I'm always afraid that I'm going to drop it on the floor and it will smash into pieces, and I'd be in for it, then.

When I find it, it's still warm. I rest my toes on it and lie there, listening. I don't hear a whole lot of noise downstairs. After the incident with the knife, I find that I can't stay in bed late, because I'd rather be aware of what's going on. I need to be able to suss out Mammy's mood, so I can make myself scarce if I need to. I put on my clothes and tiptoe down the stairs. Clare must have gone out. Daddy's in the front room reading the paper, and Mammy's in the kitchen, packing sandwiches. There doesn't seem to be much tension. It's almost worse when things are alright, because now I'll just have to wait for it to blow up.

Mammy catches sight of me and says, 'We are going for a spin.'

I find it hard to get excited, because the 'spins' often end in a drunken fight between her and Daddy.

'Sure, I'll be grand here,' I say. 'I can look after Enda.' I figure that I can manage to mind him, because I'm almost ten now. He's at home for a visit from the residential facility where he lives most of the time, and I figure that we can play for a while or maybe do some painting. Besides, anything's better than being in a confined space with the two of them.

'You're both coming with us and that's that,' Mammy replies ominously.

A while later, we're off: Mammy, Daddy, Enda and me. I don't even ask where we are heading: I just make sure I bring toys with me, because I never know how long these spins are going to go on for. Enda and I are in the back of the van. There's a blanket on the floor for us, but because there are no seats, every pothole in the road feels like a crater. There isn't a bit of padding on me, and I feel like I'm in a bumper car sometimes. I can't see out the front because there's now some plywood between the front and the rear, blocking them off from each other. I hate when I can't see where I'm going: it makes me feel dizzy, sick and very disorientated.

After ages, the van starts to slow down and now seems to be on very soft ground. Wait now… I can hear water, I think. It's waves! We must be at the beach! I can hardly contain myself. Enda squeals with excitement. *Deadly*, I think, when Mammy opens the side door and we jump out. We're parked right on a strand.

But then she grabs our hands and walks us up to the pub instead.

'You're both going to the toilet, then it's straight back out to the van,' she says, gripping our hands firmly.

I don't need to go, but I figure that I need to try and make myself go because I have a feeling this is going to be a long day for us. Daddy takes Enda into the gents' toilets. When I finish, it is straight back to the van for the two of us. I plead with Mammy to let us run on the beach for a bit to stretch our legs, but I'm wasting my time. We're ordered into the back, the sandwiches are flung in and the door slammed. I just need to give in to it, I decide wearily.

Enda and I play with the toys for a bit and munch on the sandwiches, even though I'm not hungry. I don't know how much time has passed, but I can hear the drone from the music in the pub – it sounds kind of ghostly from here. I chat away out loud to myself and Enda, while he sucks his thumb. I always explain things to him to try and keep him from getting stressed.

I don't know if it's my imagination, but the hiss of the sea seems to be getting louder. I am feeling kind of cold now. I wrap the blanket around Enda and snuggle into him to keep us both warm. I have no idea what time it is. The van is getting dark inside, and I start to feel a bit uneasy. I am bursting to go to the toilet now, but I hold it in.

I am nearly sure I feel the van wobble a bit, but it must be in my head, I think. The next thing, I see something black coming in under the side door. I freeze. 'Oh, Jesus.'

Enda can see it too, and he's getting agitated, making soft sounds of distress. I now realise that the black thing is water – the sea is coming into the van. I try to scream, but nothing comes out of my mouth. I almost feel like I'm not here now. I don't feel cold any more. I'm not bursting to go to the toilet any more. I can't even feel my own body. I am just glued to the spot, staring at the ocean coming in. I had taken my shoes off, and now the water is covering my toes. I look around to see if there's a door handle inside, but I can't find one. We're stuck. *Please God, make this go quickly*, I think. Enda is starting to slap his head with his hand the way he does when he's distressed, then he starts to scream.

Suddenly, I hear banging on the side of the van and somebody shouting, 'Is there anyone in there?' No sound will come out of my mouth, but I manage to bang back. Eventually the door slides open, and we're grabbed by the arms. A strange man pulls us out and takes us to the rocks. I look back at the van, and the water is almost halfway up, lapping over the wheel arches.

'Where are your parents?' the stranger says, looking at me with concern.

I open my mouth, but nothing will come out.

'Come on,' he says, taking us gently by the hand.

Enda and I walk barefoot into the pub. The rest of that experience is blank. I don't remember where Mammy and Daddy are in the pub, or what excuse they give to the stranger who's rescued us, but from that moment on, I have a fear of water. If I see even a leaky water pipe or an overflowing water tank, my mind returns to the van. My heart races, my mouth goes dry, and I can't speak. It takes a few moments before I can see that this is not life-threatening like it was before. That it's not fight or flight. Because Enda finds it hard to verbalise his feelings, I don't know how it's affected him, but I can't imagine that it hasn't. I wonder if, like me, he lies awake at night, seeing the water seep through the door, feeling the chill of it, knowing that at any moment, he'll drown.

CHAPTER THIRTEEN

THE DIAGNOSIS

MAMMY AND DADDY NEVER TALK ABOUT THE SPIN AGAIN. It's as if it never happened, and I wonder if this is because they were too drunk to remember or because they'd prefer to forget it. But I know that I can't forget. I don't tell a soul, though, because if it gets back to Mammy, she'll kill me.

The following week, I wake early. It's a school day and because Mammy's usually gone to work by this time, I know that I can relax. I start to get up and get dressed when my bedroom door swings open. I jump with fright. Why is Mammy still here?

She stares at me for a bit, then says, 'You'd better look neat this morning for school.' She turns on her heel and leaves the room.

I wonder why she's suddenly interested in the way I look. I always do look neat – in the mornings, anyway, and I always get myself up and out to school, when I do go. So why is she calling me for school? She doesn't usually. I feel that familiar tightness in my chest that comes whenever Mammy is around.

I'm up and dressed as quickly as I can. I grab my bag and go downstairs. Mammy is in the kitchen and she tells me to get into the van with Daddy.

'What for?' I ask.

'Because I said so,' she says, without further explanation.

I jump up beside Daddy in the van, and a few minutes later Mammy gets in. What's going on? My stomach begins to churn with anxiety. I don't ever remember them coming into the school together. *This isn't good*, I think. Maybe it's because I haven't been in school much lately.

We drive to the school in complete silence, and when we arrive, Mammy tells me to hurry up and jump down out of the van. She marches ahead while I wait for Daddy. He holds my hand as we go through the door. We're not going towards my classroom, but instead, we walk towards one of the offices. I rack my brains to work out what's going on. I don't think I'm in trouble. I didn't do much homework from the night before, but it's always like that. I can't really do the homework by myself, and there's nobody around to help me.

Yet Mammy didn't seem to be in that much of a temper with me this morning. If I was in big trouble, she would have been really angry with me. Instead, her expression is polite as she knocks on the door. It's opened by a woman I've never seen before, and my first thought is that she looks like something out of the *Rocky Horror Picture Show*. I run my eyes slowly over her black patent-leather stilettos upwards to her fishnet tights, miniskirt, tight top, blood-red nail varnish, red lipstick and a fag hanging out of her mouth. To think that I'd been told to look my best!

Of course, Daddy's eyes nearly fall out of his head. He has that expression on his face that I notice when he sees the blonde Redcoats in Butlin's. It really embarrasses me. The woman shakes Mammy's and Daddy's hands and says her name is Kathleen. I go to extend my hand, and she doesn't even look at me.

We're invited to sit down, and the talking starts over my head, something about my reading and writing. There's a pause. What is she waiting for? Then Kathleen, in a very matter-of-fact way, says, 'Aisling's mentally retarded, and it's possible she might need to go into a suitable institution.'

Each of those words is as clear as glass. The rush of blood is bursting like an ocean in my ears. All my senses go into overdrive, and my eyes dart between this woman and my parents, who are sitting, quite relaxed, in their chairs. I can't even feel the chair I'm sitting in at the moment. I seem to be floating above it. My chest tightens, and I realise I'm holding my breath again. I have a habit of doing this when I'm nervous, and it makes me feel dizzy. Next thing, I see Mammy and Daddy just shrugging their shoulders in agreement.

Suddenly, I have this image of the pool in Butlin's. I'm underwater, looking at the people above me, their outlines wobbly. I'm so close to them, yet I'm in a completely different world. My throat closes up, and I look up at Mammy and Daddy, waiting for them to say something – anything. I don't want to go to an institution. I've seen these places, and they don't look nice. Everyone in them seems to walk really slowly and have a fixed gaze about them. I know if I go there, before long I'll also have a fixed gaze.

In the *Peter and Jane* books, the parents protect and look after their kids, but instead, the adults chat away here as if I don't matter, as if they're deciding whether or not to throw out a Superser heater.

'We might be able to get some more help for Aisling in school,' Kathleen says. 'We can see then if her reading and writing improve before we make a decision.'

If just one of you bastards would ask me what's wrong, I would tell you, I think, *but not one of you has even looked at me once since I came into this office.* I pledge to myself that I'm not going into any institution. If it means I have to get that blade out of the greaseproof paper and use it, I will. And if I do survive till I'm grown up, I will always protect my loved ones fiercely.

There's silence in the van all the way home, and I know better than to say anything, but when we get home, I follow Daddy to his bedroom. 'Daddy, what's happening?' I ask.

He pulls me to him. 'Tiger, Kathleen is from the Department of Education. Mammy and I went to see her a few weeks ago.' Kathleen told Mammy and Daddy that the problem was that I find the school tests hard, I can't do my Irish, I write my letters back to front... there's more on the list but my head starts to get fuzzy, and I can't take it in.

'For your age, you should be a lot better in school,' Daddy says finally. He seems impatient. He is never usually like this with me, as if he doesn't know what the problem is. But I do. The problem with me is that I feel anxious and scared most of the time, so I can't relax enough to learn. The teachers are nice, but while school is a break from the house, I'm still always uneasy, and I can't make sense of what's in front of me. I wish I could open my mouth and tell one of the teachers what is happening at home.

PART TWO

_____

ALL ALONE

CHAPTER FOURTEEN

DADDY DIES

THE SUMMER HOLIDAYS COME NOT LONG AFTER THAT SCHOOL MEETING, and thoughts of Kathleen and institutions fade into the background. I wake up one sunny morning, and the first thing that strikes me is the eerie silence. No radio is blasting, there's no crashing around, nothing. Something's not right. I gingerly get out of bed and open the door as quietly as ever. I tiptoe out to the landing, and I hear whispers coming from downstairs. What's happening? There's never any whispering in this house. There's either no one here except a radio blaring, or someone is here, and they're snoring due to alcohol, hurling missiles or shouting. At the very least, there would be an uneasy tension.

But my gut doesn't register any of that at the moment. I creep down the first few stairs and peek through the banisters. I see Mammy in the front room with two priests. That's not good. I have no idea what it means, but it's not normal. Mammy doesn't go to Mass. Why is she whispering with priests? And what are they doing in this house?

I sneak past Daddy's room. I don't want to wake him because it feels kind of early in the morning. I walk back into my bedroom feeling a bit restless. This is a new situation, and it makes me feel sick. Different routines and experiences make me feel very confused and nervous: I don't know how to handle them or what I need to do to protect myself from the unknown. The weekly violence is something I expect, and there's a certain comfort in that pattern. Just like my little bits on the dressing table, it's a constant. I can predict it and know the outcome. Drink will be followed by shouting, blood, ambulance, guards.

I stand in the middle of my bedroom and try to stay calm. My stomach is cramping now. Eventually, the door opens slowly. I can't handle this. Normally, Mammy charges towards the door with intent and then violently swings it open to scream at me. This is so much more terrifying. She walks slowly towards me, makes no eye contact and just stands there for what seems like ages, with no expression on her face. I then hear the words that are to change my life forever.

'Daddy's dead.'

She walks out of the room.

I feel kind of serene, like I'm floating in mid-air. The dressing table's right in front of me, and it has a big round mirror on the top. I can see my reflection in it, and it's the only thing I'm aware of. I zone into this reflection and walk towards it. I stare and stare and stare into the mirror. I don't know how long I'm there for.

Suddenly, I'm woken from my trance. In the mirror, I can see the bedroom door opening again. It's Mick, our neighbour. Why is he here? He never comes over to visit. I turn to face him, and he walks towards me. He sits on the edge of the bed, looks straight up at me and asks me if I'm okay. I sit down beside him, and I have no words. Mick puts his arm around me tightly. All I can think of is how much this contact means to me. Mick just holds me. It's as if he knows exactly what I'm experiencing.

When Mick goes home, I stay sitting on my bed, trying to imagine my life without my daddy. After a while, I come downstairs. Mammy's in the kitchen and tells me to get out from under her feet. I just sit on the back wall and look at the sky, which is blue. That's where Daddy's going. I ask the clouds to be gentle with him, because he's not well.

I stay out the back until Mammy shouts at me to come back in. I had my tenth birthday six weeks ago, in July. It was lovely to have my daddy for ten years.

*

At the funeral Mass, I feel completely lost. This church gives me the creeps, because it's so huge and dark, full of shadows. I don't like the place, with people looking each other up and down to see what they are wearing and the basket being handed around every two minutes. The priest lives in two houses stuck together beside the church. What could you possibly need with all that space? It just seems very different from the stories we're learning about in religion in school. I don't see any of God's suffering here. All the same, I'm still glad of the neighbours' odds on a Sunday morning, outside our gate.

Now people start to form a straight line to shake hands with Mammy and my brothers and sisters, who are standing beside her. No one shakes my hand, maybe because I'm so much smaller than everyone else. I just feel lost. The bastards. I'm sick of not being seen. *That's my daddy in that box*, I think, looking at his coffin, *and he always saw me.* He was never too busy or angry, except when he was drunk, but I knew he would see me the next day. I remember him drinking the mixture of raw egg and milk the way he did every morning. When he'd see me, he'd wink. 'Hair of the dog, Tiger,' he'd say.

I cry very rarely, and I'm finding it hard to cry for my daddy today. I'm just numb. I find it hard to feel anything any more: I think it's been beaten out of me. There are loads of grown-ups pushing against me while they offer their condolences to Mammy. She has that blank expression on her face. She's probably after having a few brandies already. It's hard to tell if she's upset. I wonder if she'll miss Daddy too?

I've never been to a funeral before. Granny, Mammy's mammy, died a few weeks ago, but I didn't go down the country for the funeral. Mammy didn't say anything about Granny's funeral after she got back. I hope she didn't get drunk and make a show of herself. Our dog Scruffy died in the same week as Granny. She was a good old pal, a stray who'd just wandered into the house one day and stayed. She got knocked down on the main road. When I picked her up, she had blood coming out of her bum. Daddy put her in the van, and we went to the vet, but she had to put her down. *I really miss Scruffy*, I think, as people shake Mammy's hand.

In the graveyard, Daddy's coffin is lowered into the ground. Someone hands me a rose and tells me to throw it on the top of the coffin. I don't even look up to see who has given it to me. I stand on the edge of the hole, looking down. For a moment, I wish I was with him, his little Tiger. I delay throwing the rose for as long as I can, because I know this is the very last time I'll ever have any contact with my daddy. I aim as carefully as I can and drop the rose. It lands on the top of the coffin, then slides off down the side. I burst into tears. I've lost him. I feel like he's just died all over again.

The next thing I remember, I'm in the back room in the house. It's dark outside. I feel desperately alone, and I'm terrified. I begin to seriously fear for my life with just Mammy and me at home, because Clare's moving out soon. As little defence as Daddy gave, at least he took the brunt of the beatings. He was her main target. At other times, I hid behind his legs, but now that he's gone, it's just me. At least Enda is away most of the time. I know I need to stay out of her sight as much as possible. If we're going on any trips with school or if I need money for pencils or rulers or whatever, I'm not even going to ask her, in case she beats me. I don't want to draw any attention to myself at all.

I remember that a while back we went to Bray on a school trip. I didn't even bother telling anyone at home, because Mammy would be giving out about the cost of the coach. That morning, I made a cheese sandwich and wrapped it in tinfoil. I got the money for the coach from my piggy bank. It was fabulous going off on our adventure. There was great excitement. Everyone was munching away on their goodies, and some of my schoolmates offered me sweets. I kept saying I was grand. I would have loved to have bought sweets, but I didn't have any more money left after I paid for the coach. Anyway, I was happy enough with my cheese sambo.

When we got to the sea, everyone jumped off the coach to go across to the amusement arcade with the other teacher. I didn't like the sound coming from the arcade. It reminded me a little of Butlin's and the echoey sounds from the music in the bar, so I stayed on the coach and curled up at the back, hoping the teacher wouldn't notice I was there. She did, though, and came down the aisle with that soft, gentle smile of hers. I had no choice but to admit I had no money. She took out her purse and gave me some. I couldn't believe it. I legged it into the arcade and went straight on the ghost train. I was so happy.

Now I realise that I just need to hold tight. I'm ten now, and in six more years I'll be out of this house. I'm never going to ask any friends into the house again – not that I did much, anyway, because I didn't want the embarrassment of them seeing Mammy falling in the door or shouting at them. I'll have my bath at the weekend, I decide, after she leaves for the pub. It can be one thing I can do inside and feel safe, because she took the handle off the bathroom door recently, so she can just walk in. Sometimes, when I'm going to the toilet, she comes in and laughs. I don't know whether it's to humiliate me or something else. Mammy isn't just hot-tempered and cruel: there seems to be something else wrong with her. She's just not right in the head.

CHAPTER FIFTEEN

THE VISION

DADDY HAS BEEN GONE A WEEK NOW. I hope he's in heaven looking down on me. I don't go to Mass, but I do believe in God, or some kind of higher being anyway, up in the sky. I talk to this power in the sky all the time. At times I plead with this God to get me through the night safely, now that Daddy's gone. I say the prayer, 'And if I die before I wake, I pray to God my soul to take.' Eventually, I drift off for a bit, my body still alert for any noise from downstairs. Mammy has been drinking ever since the funeral, and she's gone completely off her head, shouting and crashing about until the early hours of the morning.

Then, something out of this world happens. All of a sudden, I'm awake and I'm pulled from the bed up to one corner of the bedroom. I look down on myself in the bed for maybe one or two seconds, then I'm catapulted violently back down on to the bed. I lie awake for the rest of the night, trying to make sense of what just happened. I don't feel serene or enlightened. It just felt so bloody real. I wonder if it was Daddy, showing me that he was still there, sending me some kind of message. It does give me a little bit of hope, though. If ever I had doubts, I know now there is something out there, and this gives me enough reason to want to live and give this life my best shot. As dawn breaks, I take the blade out of the greaseproof paper, where I've kept it for so many years, and drop it down between the floorboards. I'm here for a reason and I'm staying.

The funny thing is that after that experience, I meet the woman who will be one of the most important people in my life. Sometimes I wonder if Daddy sent her to look after me. It happens when I go back to school after the summer holidays. It's a week after Daddy died, and I'm really glad to be back because I need some kind of routine or a constant like never before.

I'm now in fourth class. I'm still sitting by the window, where I can gaze out and daydream. I didn't see a lot of the girls in the class over the holidays, and they don't know about Daddy. There's great excitement among most of them, catching up and talking about where they went on their holidays and so on. I settle quietly into my seat, comforted by the fact that it is in the same place that it was when I left in June. I was hoping it would be safe while I wasn't there.

Suddenly, among all the chatter, the teacher calls my name, discreetly and gently. I look up and she asks me, 'Aisling, what did your father like to be called? Jimmy or James?' I notice she has a Mass card in her hand.

Well, I sit up like a proud cockerel and say, 'James.' Oh, it feels so lovely to say his name. It makes me feel as if he's been brought to life again. The teacher hands me the card, and I leave it on my desk under my copybook. Every now and then, I stroke it tenderly. At big break, I can't help but open the card and run my finger slowly over Daddy's name, again and again. I've never had this feeling of pride before. I feel a real sense of achievement when I manage to do a good freehand drawing of, say, a horse, but this is so different. This is something real. Something I can feel with my Daddy's name on it. I loved the sound of his name when the teacher said it. I love how his name looks on the card. I don't think I'll ever forget this.

The weather is getting cooler now, and we're heading into the winter. I don't mind, though. My hands aren't as shaky as they usually are when I'm asked a question. I pretend that Daddy's with me all the time. It's great, because no one else can see him, except me. When Mammy loses her temper now, I'm able to protect and hide Daddy. He should really have died sooner: that way, I would have been able to mind him for longer.

A few months later, during break time, my teacher asks me to follow her to the girls' school. I don't know what she wants, but I'm excited. Then we walk towards one of the offices. I immediately recognise the door. It is the very office where Mammy and Daddy were told, only a while ago, that I was mentally retarded. I freeze. It's always been in the back of my head that someone is going to collect me and lock me up. *Maybe this is it*, I think. Maybe Kathleen has come for me again.

I'm reluctant to go in, but the teacher says, 'Go ahead, Aisling, it's okay.'

She shows me into the office, and I stop holding my breath when I see that it's safe. There's no sign of Kathleen. 'Would you like to sit beside me?' my teacher asks. She looks me right in the eyes. Her eyes are green, just like mine. My teacher explains to me that she's going to be doing some remedial teaching soon. I don't know what she means. She goes on to explain that instead of teaching a class, she's going to help me and other children with our learning.

Nervously, I sit down. 'Now, let's play a game of bingo,' she says, pulling out two sheets with numbered boxes on them and placing one in front of me. I don't know what bingo has to do with reading and writing, but that doesn't matter at all, because it's fun. I score a full house, and she says that I'm very clever. Actually, it doesn't matter what she does with me. I can't believe how lucky I am. My teacher tells me that it's going to take another little while before these sessions are set up, but when they are, every week, at the same time, I'll go to this same office, and my teacher will be there, waiting to greet me. I've never known anything like this before. The idea that I have sacred, undisturbed time with an adult with whom I can feel completely safe is hard to comprehend. Here is a grown-up who isn't relying on me to mind her, like Mammy sometimes does, to try to stop her from choking after one of her sessions. Instead, this grown-up is spending this precious time every week with me.

It takes me a while to trust this routine, because I don't think it's going to happen the following week, and then it does. Soon, I learn that my teacher is here for me every week, just like she said she would be. And at the end of each session, she tells me exactly what we're going to do the following week. That really calms me down. I don't have to feel nervous about coming next time, because I'll have an idea of what's ahead. There'll be no horrible surprises. In my world, surprises are never nice.

I start to feel a sense of pride in myself. I walk straighter, and for the first time in my life, I'm aware of my body and how little space I've been taking up in the world. Up to now, the only thing I could focus on was staying out of sight and being as quiet as possible. Now, in spite of Daddy's death, something has shifted in me. My teacher has given me self-worth. She encourages me and relies on me to be there also. This gives me a different type of responsibility: a responsibility to myself to make it to these sessions. I am now starting to feel worthy of being here on this planet, just like everyone else. I see myself differently in the mirror. Before long, my reading and writing start to improve.

One day, I arrive as usual, ready to sit down and practise my reading, and my teacher says, 'Aisling, would you mind helping me to set the table for some other pupils, because you don't need to come for extra lessons any more.'

'But I thought they were putting me in an institution,' I protest.

'Nobody is going to put you in an institution,' my teacher says, 'because you're now as good as everyone else.' I feel so, so proud and want to burst with joy. I decide that today is the best day of my life.

When the bell rings at the end of the day, I run home, dying to tell Mammy my news when she gets in from work later on. It might make her happy, I think, to know that I've done so well. After running breathlessly through the back door, I come across Mammy in the kitchen. She must have a day off, because she isn't usually home until the evening. I blurt out my news, while she raises a cup of tea to her lips. Without notice, the mug comes flying in my direction and smashes against the back door. I run straight out to the back garden and wait for ages until it's safe to go back inside. *It doesn't matter what Mammy does*, I think. I can take comfort in my achievement in school. I'm aware that this experience is sending me on a new path. My teacher has instilled in me a new faith in humans and some day, when I have the right words, I will thank her.

CHAPTER SIXTEEN

CYCLING THE BORDER

WITH DADDY GONE, Mammy has to get on with the practical tasks around the house, as well as her job. It's one of the things I actually admire about her – her skill with a screwdriver and a saw. She doesn't complain about the DIY jobs, she just gets on with them, and she's even shown me how to do them. Sometimes she can be like that, almost nice, but I know better than to trust that she'll stay that way.

Today, it's been a year and a half since Daddy died. I'm now eleven, and it's not long since I finished my one-to-one lessons with my teacher. I'm feeling so much more confident. I can read and write well now, and everything that had looked so unfamiliar on the blackboard is beginning to make sense. But when Mammy suggests that we go to Newry to buy a new bicycle for me and a lawn-mower to replace the one that's been broken, I'm wary. I don't want to be stuck with her in a car for a whole two hours there and back.

My black bike was stolen outside the front of the house a few months ago. I left it out the front one day while I ran in to get something, and when I came out, it was gone. I went down to the Garda station to tell them, but sure, what were they going to be able to do about it? Funnily enough, Mammy didn't kill me when I told her; she just said nothing. I was astonished, but maybe she thought that losing my bike was lesson enough. I loved that bike. It was only my second bike ever. I remember clearly the day I learned to cycle. It was a Sunday. I reckon I must have been about seven. When I saw Daddy coming out to the back garden with that little red bike, I couldn't believe it. I was so happy and surprised. It had stabilisers on it. I'll never forget that freeing sensation of sitting on it and zooming around. Daddy helped me go around in little circles until finally I got the hang of it. It gave me tingles of excitement.

The stabilisers came off after about a week because I just cycled non-stop around the garden, so I learned to ride pretty quickly. I fell off it about twenty times in the process, I'd say. When I grew out of that bike, which was second-hand, I got the black one. It didn't have a cross-bar, which I preferred, because my legs were short, so I could step through. I really miss it. Since then, I've used Mammy's old black bike, a big thing with huge wheels and a basket on the front. It's like something out of a World War II film. It's kind of heavy to cycle, and there are no gears, but I like that it feels quite safe.

I've had some deadly cycles on Black Bess, as I call her. Only a while ago, myself and my mates went down to the Strawberry Beds on our bikes. We cycled through the Phoenix Park and came out at the top of the hill that leads down to the Liffey. The idea was that we'd whizz down it on our bikes. It's really steep and narrow, and I'd never been down it on a bicycle before, but I was up for it. I'm always up for an adventure.

Even though there wasn't much traffic on the road, we said we'd go down in turns, because we knew it wouldn't be that easy to control the bikes, and we didn't want to crash into each other. I decided to go down last, so I could learn from the mistakes of the others. As it turned out, it wasn't a whole lot of benefit to me. I braced myself and pushed myself off slowly, but the bike very quickly picked up momentum. It wasn't long before I started to lose control of it. Lately, I had noticed that there was a slight bump in the front tyre, and that made the bike quite unstable as it picked up speed. It was now time to very gently squeeze the brakes. So, do you think the brakes worked? Not at all!

There I was, bombing down the Strawberry Beds on Black Bess with no brakes and a hump on the front wheel. I used to think I'd be found dead at the hands of my mother, but I now had visions of myself landing in a ditch with a bike wrapped around my neck. The bike seemed to be getting faster and faster. Towards the end of the hill, I lost control completely, and the bike came off the road and into the river. I went over the handlebars and landed right on my knees. It was only when I stood up that I felt the sting. Both my knees were completely grazed, blood streaming down my shins. I didn't mind the blood, but I didn't like having to pick out all the bits of grit from my knees. The rest of the gang were all on the bank having a great laugh. I pulled the bike out of the water, which wasn't a problem, because the river was very shallow at that end, since it was just before the weir. That was deadly craic, I have to say. One of the lads threw me an apple. I took a bite, and we headed back up the hill.

I'm thinking about this as Mammy and I sit in the car together, whizzing northwards. I've never gone very far in the car with her, so the usual nerves kick in about being with her in a confined space. She turns the radio up loud, which for once suits me because it means we're not going to talk – not that we ever do, really – but it still hurts my ears. I have a tissue in my pocket. I tear off a couple of pieces, roll them up and stick one in each ear. My left ear hurts when I push it in, and I wince with the pain. It's been sore since Mammy started to beat me about the head. I've also started getting bad headaches on the right side of my head and bright flashing lights hurt my eyes.

The road from Dublin to Newry is the same all the way up, a series of bumps and potholes all over the place. Mammy tears up the road in silence, the radio blaring. I look at her face, which is freshly powdered, the lipstick on her lips bright. For once, her face isn't dark with anger, or loose and sloppy with drink.

'Mammy?'

'What?' she replies sharply, but she's not looking too angry, so I persist.

'How did you meet Daddy?'

I wonder if her face will darken at the mention of his name, but instead, she gives a small smile. 'Well, I'd come up to Dublin to work, and I was out for a walk one day when I bumped into Daddy, and he asked me out.'

'Just like that?' I say, trying to imagine Mammy and Daddy on a footpath somewhere in Dublin, chatting like two normal people.

'Just like that,' she replies. 'In those days, it wasn't complicated. If you met someone you liked, you went out with them and then you got married and had a family.'

There's a short pause while I think about this, before Mammy adds, 'We lived with Daddy's parents when we got married, you know.'

I've never really heard her talk about Daddy's mother and father. Mammy didn't keep in contact with Daddy's family, so I have no idea who my cousins, aunts and uncles are on that side.

'Oh, yes. They lived in a huge house,' she adds. 'When we bought our own house and moved in, it was like moving into a matchbox.'

Our house isn't small, so I try to imagine how big Daddy's house was. I think of a big red-brick mansion with turrets and a big lawn. 'Was Daddy rich?'

'His family were well-to-do,' Mammy replies. I don't really know what that means, but I can't help wondering where all the money went.

'What about your family?' I ask. I know that Mammy comes from a big family, but when I've asked about them before, all she'll say is that her brother lives over-seas and the rest of her family live in the country. I've always thought it a bit strange that she doesn't see them any more. Even though I'm the youngest, I hope that I won't ever lose contact with my brothers and sisters. She does keep in touch with a nephew of hers, and he and his wife have called into the house a couple of times. They're lovely, and I wonder if they know what Mammy's really like.

'What about them?' she replies.

'I wondered what it was like growing up in the country,' I say.

'It was fine,' she says briefly. Then she turns up the radio, and I know that the conversation is closed. Still, it's rare for Mammy and me to have a normal conversa-tion at all, so I'm quite surprised and glad about that.

When we finally get to Newry, she runs into a news-agent's and asks where she'd find a hardware shop. He gives her directions, and when we get there, she means business. There's no hanging around. She knows exactly what she wants: a brand-new self-drive lawnmower. She'll pay for her lawnmower in cash, and off we'll go. I have to say, I admire that about her. She seems to be very independent in that way. When she wants something, she just goes for it. She doesn't seem to ask other people for advice. Mammy knows her own mind. She probably got that from Granny.

I think about the day, not long ago, when Mammy brought me into town to leave her fur coat in storage for the summer. Mammy had a few fur coats, and in order for them not to get eaten by moths, she'd bring them into Switzers department store on Grafton Street, where they were stored in a big freezer until wintertime. Mammy loves Switzers, but I didn't see why I had to go with her. Still, she bought me an ice-cream cone, and that cheered me up a bit. We headed for Switzers, and Mammy told me to sit and wait for her at the end of the big staircase in the middle of the shop. I was sitting to one side of the steps and was happy enough just watching people milling around, looking at this and that. The ice cream was gor-geous, really creamy, and I enjoyed every sweet mouthful. The next thing I knew, this woman swished past me in her full-length fur coat as I dipped my head to have another lick. I looked down at my empty cone. 'What the hell?' I turned my head and watched my lovely ice cream dripping off the hem of the woman's coat. I made myself scarce for a few minutes in case Mammy caught sight of me. After a while, I took up my position again and had a chuckle to myself.

In the hardware shop, Mammy examines the rows of lawnmowers. The one she wants looks deadly, and I can just see Mammy pushing it along in the garden. It's a big bulky thing, but the shop assistant eventually gets it into the car, after lots of manoeuvring. Then Mammy asks him where we can find a bike shop. I think I'm hearing things! I know she said we were getting a bike, but I didn't believe her. We walk along the street and into this bike shop, and I think I'm going to faint with excitement. I look at all the bikes lined up against the wall, all shiny and new.

'Just go and pick one out,' Mammy says.

Is this a joke? I think. Well, I'll go along for the craic, anyway, I decide. My eye is drawn to a silver racer. The crest on the front axle, under the curved handlebars, says 'British Eagle'. It has a crossbar, but it's not actually too big, and I can just see myself on it, racing along. I tell her that this is the one.

'Right,' she says, reaching into her handbag and producing a wad of notes. *Am I in some kind of a dream?* I wonder.

We wheel the bike out, and it very quickly dawns on her that she won't be allowed to get both these items through the border controls, which are very strict at the moment. My heart sinks. I know that if she has to choose between the bike and the lawnmower, the lawnmower will win. I knew it was too good to be true. My daydreams of racing along on my new bike aren't going to come true.

She thinks for a bit, then she says, 'Right, you're just going to have to cycle around the border checkpoint.'

I'm eleven. I'm miles away from home. I can't understand maps. The signposts in this country all seem to point in the opposite direction to the way they're meant to, and my mother sends me off to tour the countryside! Then I decide that there's nothing else for it: if I want my bike, I'll have to ride it.

'You'll need to find a crossing with no border guards on it,' Mammy instructs me. 'And when you see a car, flag it down and ask for directions to the Dublin Road. We'll meet at the petrol station nearest the border checkpoint.'

I jump on my saddle and head for a side road that I hope leads to an unmanned bit of the border. If I do get to the main road, I'll just have to keep asking people for directions to the petrol station. Thank God it's not pissing rain.

I feel excitement and terror at the same time. These lads have guns! It's no joke. I now go into my fantasy world and pretend that I'm a fugitive from prison. I am shaking, but after a while I kind of calm down a bit when I realise that this can only go one of two ways: I'll be caught or I won't be caught. Mammy said that if she didn't see me in an hour and a half she'd get on to border control and sort it out then. I take her word for it that she'll be at the garage waiting for me. I don't really have much option.

I've never had gears on a bike before, and it feels so strange. As I'm pedalling along, I'm fascinated by how thin the tyres are. The handlebars are brilliant, though, curled under in the proper racing style. I crouch right down, raise my ass and now I'm in my element. I'm on a real-life adventure. I'm not afraid now. I have to stop a couple of times and ask people to point me in the right direction, to the South, which they do, even if they look a bit surprised. After an hour or so, I get to what I think is the main road. It's a lot bigger than the ones I've just left, anyway. I go with my gut and pedal towards the afternoon sun. Finally, thank God, I see a garage. Yes, that's the one. If she's left without me, I'm finished. No way, I see a car! On closer inspection, I realise that it's Mammy's: there's a familiar dent on the front left panel, where she scraped along our gate recently.

When I get there, she's inside, paying for petrol. When she sees me, she says, 'About fucking time.'

It takes us a while to get the bike into the back of Mammy's little car along with the lawnmower. In the end, we have to put the back seats down and keep the boot open for the rest of the journey. I climb into the front seat and hold on tightly to the front wheel of the bike all the way home.

A few evenings later, I'm hanging around the school-yard, showing the bike off to a few of the lads, and I'm discreetly advised to get rid of the crest on the front. I didn't even think of that. I just loved the look of that crest.

CHAPTER SEVENTEEN

FALLING APART

MY SENSE OF SECURITY IS SHORT-LIVED, THOUGH. As it always does, a switch flips in Mammy, and her behaviour changes again. Sometimes, I wish that I knew how to predict these sudden shifts in mood, but I don't. With Daddy and my brother and sister now gone, and Enda in his residential home, Mammy is like a car without brakes: out of control. She goes out to the pub every night, and most nights she doesn't come home alone. I get used to the bang of the front door as it swings open, the thump of bodies as they fall in on to the hall stairs. There's exaggerated whispering and cackling from Mammy as they climb the stairs, while I lie frozen in the bed. I've also got used to not sleeping for more than a few minutes at a time, even if it means I spend my day in school nodding off over my desk. I've got bags under my eyes, I'm always really pale and I don't have the energy to concentrate.

Tonight, I am in my bed, curled up with Panda. His leg is getting flat from my head lying on it every night. I love to look up at his face. I always feel like he's cradling me. We look after each other, Panda and me. When I'm in bed, he minds me as best he can, and whenever I'm not home, I always tuck him in safely, so he doesn't fall out. It's a single bed, and Panda takes up a good chunk of it.

I'm startled by the front door opening. I'm such a light sleeper. The second I hear a noise, I'm alert, ready to jump out of bed if I have to. There's now a muffled sound that seems to go on for ages. I sit up in bed, my back against the wall, and I take Action Man out, so I can try and go into my fantasy world. It's not working this time, because I can still hear someone on the stairs. It's not Mammy. It's a heavy step. It's slow and sneaky. I jump back under the covers and pretend to be asleep. The door opens really slowly.

I smell him first, the stench of fags and drink sticking in the air. My light is off, but there's a full moon outside, and it's casting some light through the window, enough for me to open an eyelid very slightly to see a big bulk of a man standing over me. My face is about six inches away from the front of his thighs. He then slowly moves my blankets down and gets into bed beside me. My back is now touching the cold wall. I can feel his whole body pressed against me. My head is stuck in his chest. I want to pass out with the smell. I am aware that Mammy is downstairs and hope against all odds that she comes up to save me. Yet I know at the same time that that's not going to happen.

When he's finished hurting me inside, he asks me if I like dresses. I almost turn into a baby. I say, 'Yeah.'

'What colour dresses do you like? Pink or blue?' he asks.

'Pink.' What the hell am I saying? I hate pink! I think I've turned myself into a toddler, so the real Ais doesn't need to deal with it.

The man doesn't seem to be in a big hurry to get out of the bed, and he doesn't seem afraid that he'll be caught. I wonder at that moment, if I had kept that razor blade instead of slipping it between the floorboards, whether I would have used it on him. He pulls down the blankets and walks out.

I just lie there and think about other promises that were made by some of the men who come home with Mammy from the pub and who sneaked into my bed late at night. It's a bit blurry, but there have been a good few of them. I remember one of them promised he'd collect me one Sunday morning and take me to the horse show at the RDS to see Eddie Macken and Harvey Smith, my showjumping heroes. I couldn't wait to go and didn't sleep the night before with excitement. When the Sunday came, I waited by the front door. I must have stayed there for hours, but the man never came. My heart was broken. A few days later, I wrote to *Jim'll Fix It* to see if Jimmy Savile could help me to meet my two heroes. In hindsight, I'm glad that one didn't happen.

I'm not shocked or surprised by these night-time visits, even though I'm scared. I've always known somewhere inside of me that Mammy wouldn't protect me in the way Daddy did. He may not have been able to stand up to her, but I'm sure that he wouldn't have let this happen. Without anyone to help me, I feel completely alone. I can't tell anyone because I feel too embarrassed. I can see my teacher's kind face, her green eyes sparkling as she gives me another task and praises me for completing it. I wonder what she would do if I told her.

The worst night comes later, when Mammy brings home two of them.

Again, I'm in bed, half-asleep. There are suddenly a lot of voices in the house, and I listen carefully, trying to work out how many. I can hear Mammy's voice and the deeper ones of what sounds like two men. I'm terrified. I pray and pray and pray that they won't come upstairs, but soon, I hear two heavy sets of feet on the stairs.

Then the door opens. Two men come in. One is very stocky, with a beard and moustache; the other looks neater. The heavier one walks towards my bed with a smile on his face and says, 'Hi.' The other one is standing by the door. It's slightly ajar. He's peeking out, keeping sketch. This scares me more than the others for some reason. I feel a loneliness like never before. Mammy is downstairs. She came into this house with those two men. She must realise they're not with her by now, unless she's passed out. That happens a lot these days.

The one at the door seems to be the 'talker'. He commands me, 'Do whatever it is he wants you to do.'

I want to die now. *I hate you, God*, I think. *I hate you.*

The big heavyset man is lying on top of me. It doesn't take long before I start to feel pain. A searing pain. I keep thinking of the razor blade. I've often fantasised about slitting my wrists and wondered what it would feel like physically. Now I feel like there's a giant razor blade slicing me open, from my groin to my neck. My eyes are fixed on my wallpaper. I have wood-chip wallpaper, and I love picking out the little pieces of wood chip from the paper when I'm stressed. I always imagine they're little people. The ones that are tucked safely behind the paper are the goodies. The ones that I pick out from time to time are the baddies. Some of the edges of the wallpaper are frayed. I focus on a frayed edge, manage to reach for it and grab it with my fingers. I hold on to it tightly and slowly pull that piece from the wall. When I set myself a task, I like to stick with it. Everything is measured, so that I have some kind of control, a process that gets me from one step to the next. Now I tell myself to pull it slowly, so that by the time the piece of wallpaper comes off the wall completely, it'll all be over. I lose my bet. He squashes my body under his weight just before I finish my task. I can't breathe. I'm going to suffocate. He eventually goes away, and I feel nothing.

CHAPTER EIGHTEEN

THE TRAVELLERS

'VE NEVER NEEDED THE OPEN AIR AS MUCH AS I DO NOW. A space where I can't be trapped like an animal in a cage, at risk of being attacked at any moment. I even go to the toilet outside, because I can't go when I'm in the bathroom in case Mammy bursts in. Even though I'm twelve and I really need privacy, she can come in at any minute, because there's no longer a lock on the door.

The only bright spot in my life at the moment comes from my grown-up friends by the canal. They're Travellers, and they are always very good to me. I like to think that they understand me, and I understand them. One of them, an old woman called Bridget, knocks on our door every Thursday. My brother Sean used to make her a cheese sandwich and a glass of milk, so I do too, and we sit together out the front on the garden bench and chat.

A few weeks ago, I asked Bridget where she lived and about her family. She told me they lived up on the canal and that I could go up and join them at the fire. This sounded brilliant, to sit around a warm fire, looking into the crackling flames, with nice people, listening to their stories. Eventually, going up to see the Travellers became a regular thing.

The last time I was up, I asked them if they needed a pot or a pan. I was thinking that if I got rid of a pot or a pan, that would be one less piece of ammunition for Mammy to use on me. Since Clare left home, I've felt like an open target, and I'd be gone too, if I could. I really miss Clare, even though she does her best to keep an eye on me. At Christmas, she got the bus down from her place and called in for me to take me to Funderland. I just loved the rides, especially the Wall of Death. How the rider stayed on his bike going around the wall, I'll never know. My favourite was the themed photo studio. Clare and I went through all the costumes, and we decided we'd dress up in Victorian clothing to have our pictures taken. I was a man, which goes without saying. The costume was fab: I got to wear a top hat and tails, just like Daddy when he was young. Clare looked great in her dress and flouncy hat. I still have that photo. I treasure it.

There's one pan in particular that terrifies me. It's an old black cast-iron one that weighs a ton. If Mammy hit me with it, I'd be gone in an instant. One evening, I take it out of the oven and go out the back to head up to the Travellers' site. I place the pan carefully on top of the wall. If this thing falls on me, it's going to split my skull. 'Grand.' I now have it safely in my hands. Up the road I go.

I get to the bridge, and when I see the bonfire, I immediately feel like I'm home. As I get closer, I give them a wave. There are three caravans parked right on the canal bank, and when I look at them, I feel envious. Their freedom is everything I crave. When Bridget sees me, she beckons me over. The crackling fire and the smell of burning sticks relax me instantly. I love the smell of bonfire on my clothes. It comforts me.

Bridget has an old black teapot hanging over the fire on a hook. I'm offered a mug of tea, and Maureen, Bridget's daughter, hands it to me in a metal cup. I hand over the frying pan and think to myself, *Good riddance.*

Bridget says, 'God bless you,' and puts the pan carefully down. As we sit by the fire, we don't say much, but I feel so comfortable in that space. I feel like I've known them a lot longer than I have. I finish the tea, and Bridget asks if I want to go into a caravan so she can read my palm. I'm not sure I believe in that kind of thing, but I don't hesitate. 'Yes please,' I say. Maybe Bridget might tell me when I'll be able to get away from Mammy.

The caravan is tiny, but it feels safe and cosy. Bridget sits opposite me and takes my palm in hers. She examines it carefully and tells me bits and bobs that I don't take much heed of. But when she tells me my lifeline is broken, I start to listen a bit better. 'You won't reach old age,' she says softly, peering at the broken line. 'You won't be too sick up to that point, but you'll die young.' I don't ask her how old we're talking about, because I don't want to know. There always seems to be a battle with me between living and dying. I've spent so long wanting to die, but since Daddy died, in spite of everything that's happened, I want to live. And not just exist, like he did: I want to grab life by the balls and experience it, all of it, the good bits and the bad bits. I feel like I've got a head start with the bad bits, anyway, so maybe it'll all be good from now on.

I need to head home, because if Mammy finds out where I've been, she'll eat me alive. I'm halfway home, and the reality of taking the frying pan hits me. She's going to kill me when she finds out. I won't say anything, I decide. She's going to keep hitting me, anyway, so I don't give a damn. I don't even feel it any more. Something in me has shifted slightly with Mammy. I'm not cheeky with her; I don't answer back. I just seem to have got better at evading her, and even when I don't manage to dodge her, the beatings don't seem as painful as they were.

Mammy's behaviour, on the other hand, is getting worse. She's started drinking in the mornings when she's not at work, and this makes things even more frightening. When she goes out in the evening, she comes home very angry but eventually goes to bed, which means I get a break for two or three hours towards the morning. But when she goes out drinking early in the day, the afternoon is really scary. The evening is even more scary, because she nods off but wakes up on and off, screaming and demanding things, and she just doesn't settle at all.

Now, I'm coming out of my bedroom, and I meet her coming out of her room. I nearly wet myself when we meet in the middle. How did I mess that up? It's so unlike me. She's about to do something now, I know, but I'm saved by a knock on the door. Mammy peers down the stairs and says, 'Fuck, whoever it is, tell them I'm not in.' I can see a shadow through the glass. I casually go downstairs, open the door and matter-of-factly say, 'Mammy told me to tell you that she's not in.'

Next thing, she tears down the stairs, shoves me aside and apologises to the caller, an insurance seller. After she talks to him nicely for a couple of minutes and tells him that she doesn't need insurance, the man goes away. She closes the door, gets hold of me, makes a fist with her hand and slams it into the side of my head. I look at her and start to laugh. I shouldn't, but I don't know what's got into me. I wait for her to completely beat the shit out of me, but she doesn't. Just for a moment, I feel as if I have the upper hand. I'm now the same height as Mammy and I can look her right in the eye. Maybe she might be a little nervous of me now.

I should have known better, though. Later on that day, she tells me we're going for a drive. I just give in to it, because I know better than to argue. Her driving scares me, though. I don't think she's ever had lessons, and she has her own rules. She's always hitting other people's cars when she's parking, and it doesn't seem to bother her. Thankfully, after about an hour, we get to wherever we were going in one piece. It looks really depressing, grey and drab. I have no idea where we are.

Mammy stops the car. 'I have to see a man about a dog,' she says.

I wonder if we're getting a new dog.

We park beside a statue that looks like St Anthony. I'm not sure, because I've never spent any time inside a church. There's a little brown suitcase at the foot of the statue, and it looks really old. Mammy tells me she'll be back in a while. She walks into the pub across the road. I'm happy enough here. I stay by the statue for ages, trying to figure out what the story is with the suitcase. I'd love to open it, but I decide not to. Instead, I bring the statue alive in my mind's eye and I chat away to it, about this and that. I conclude that the statue must have travelled from somewhere particularly dismal to shack up here. At least it's not raining.

After a while, Mammy comes out of the pub and tells me, 'We're going to the church to say a prayer: you need to cleanse yourself.' She nods her head in the direction of the little church behind the statue. This doesn't feel natural to me. Mammy isn't religious, and apart from Daddy's funeral, she hasn't been to Mass in years. I always chat to God in Murph's field, or when I'm watching the sunset, so I don't need to pray in church. I don't like churches, because they give me the creeps.

When we go in, it's eerily quiet, and there isn't another soul around. Candles are flickering in the draught from the half-open door.

Mammy eyes the confession box in the corner. 'We'll have pretend confession,' she says. 'I'll be the priest, and we'll both get into the box.'

I'm surprised at Mammy wanting to play a game like this, but I'm up for it. It might be a bit of craic, I figure. Once I'm inside the box, I wait for Mammy to settle herself on the priest's side of the confessional. Instead, I hear what sounds like a large object being dragged across the floor, followed by her manic laughter and a loud thud on the confessional door. She shouts, 'See you, now. I'm going home,' her laughter getting fainter as she walks away.

It takes me a minute or two to figure this one out in my head. Why is it I don't ever see this coming? How does she still manage to fool me like this? I realise for the first time that she's really deranged. I hear the car engine starting. She's revving the engine out of it, so I know for sure that's her. She wouldn't drive off, would she?

But she does.

My chest gets tight, and I feel like I can't breathe. I open my mouth like a goldfish to suck in some air but can't seem to get enough of it. I begin to panic, before telling myself that I can either stay here or get out. I push and push and push against whatever Mammy has put against the door. Nothing's budging. I look out of the little window in the door with the velvet curtain pulled across it. *I'd never fit through it, would I?* I wonder. It's worth a try.

I place one foot on the kneeler, the other on the armrest and stick my head and shoulders through the space in the door. Eventually, I manage to pull myself through and fall down, head first, on to the big wooden pew that Mammy pushed up against the door. I'm exhausted with stress. It's at times like this that my will gets so weak. I don't have the energy to fight any more, and I just want to give in. 'Fuck you, God,' I say as I walk out of the church and up the street, to where, I don't know. I feel so disorientated, and the ringing in my ears is deafening me with its volume, the way it does when I get stressed.

Suddenly, I hear that familiar sound, as her little car roars to a stop beside me. She bends her head down and opens the passenger-side window. 'Come on, I thought you'd never come out.' It's as if she was simply waiting for me to come out of the sweet shop, not from the confession box into which she'd locked me. Silently, I get into the passenger seat.

As we're driving home, I can't help thinking about the statue with the battered suitcase. I'd give anything to pack a case and leave right now.

CHAPTER NINETEEN

STILETTOS

FTER THE INCIDENT IN THE CONFESSION BOX, Mammy's behaviour becomes increasingly bizarre and unpredictable. She comes and goes at all hours, and when she's not drunk, she's lashing out at me. I take refuge in art, drawing and painting whenever I get the chance. I reckon I have about 30 drawings now, charcoal copies of famous paintings. I also do lots of horses because I really love them and because they remind me of Daddy. Every time I watch the start of *Black Beauty*, with the horse galloping across the fields, I always imagine that's me, wild and free, with not a care in the world. I love the sense of danger that the image conjures up in my mind. It's funny, because I don't like to take risks much. There's enough danger in my life as it is.

I only work on my drawings when Mammy's not here, because I can't relax when she is. But then, sometimes I can't relax when she's out, because I'm just waiting for her to come back home again. It's all about timing. It has to be just right. If I can get started when she's leaving the house, then I know I'll have at least four hours to get stuck into drawing or dressing up or whatever before she comes home.

Now she's gone to the pub for the afternoon, and I say to myself, 'An exhibition, that's what I'll have.' I see them sometimes in films. I'll have my own exhibition and pretend I'm a famous artist. I go under the stairs and dig out all my drawings. They're all just loose, and I think that I should really keep them somewhere a bit safer. The whole lot is brought into the front room. When I feel the weight of them under my arm, I feel kind of proud of myself. I place all the drawings on the floor and get a fluffy feeling in my stomach. I feel so excited and spend ages figuring out which ones to put where. I arrange, then rearrange. Eventually, the whole front-room carpet is covered with my drawings. The oatmeal-coloured carpet is perfect as a neutral background, the ink stain barely visible now. I sit down and feel very happy with myself. For a fleeting moment, I imagine showing Mammy my little exhibition, but I'd never chance it. She would just slag me off. I don't care, though: I love drawing and painting, and I'm always going to do it. Art takes me away to somewhere calm, and it stops the headaches that seem to be coming more regularly these days. I'll be going to secondary school later this year, and I think that when I leave, I'll go to art college and learn how to be a better artist.

I pour myself a drink of lemonade and settle into the chair, something I very rarely do. If I do sit in a chair downstairs, it's always on the edge. As I'm scanning each drawing, looking at good bits and bits that could be improved, I hear the key in the door. 'No, it's too early!' I wail. I don't even have time to switch off the lights and pretend there's no one in the room, because I left the door open, and she can see the light streaming into the hallway. *Oh, please God. Just make her go straight up to bed.*

Instead, she marches into the front room and tramples over all my drawings. She's wearing stilettos. She digs her heels into each drawing, all the while sneering, 'You think you're some kind of artist.' I plead with her to get off them. All my hours of work are being ruined. The tears just drip off my face, but I'm otherwise expressionless. It's beyond my comprehension that anybody could be so cruel. As I count the holes pierced through my drawings, as if someone shot arrows through them, I vow that, unless she chops my fucking hands off, she will never stop me from drawing.

A couple of days later, I was out the back, sitting on the swing. I made sure to face the kitchen window, watching out for signs of activity, because she went out early this morning and that's never a good sign. While I was on the swing, I could keep an eye on the front door through the window, the sunlight changing direction through the glass as it opened. *Oh, no, she's back already*, I thought as I ran towards the house. I crept along the side wall, just like a spy. I moved the stepladder, which had been left underneath the kitchen window, up beside the window as quietly as possible and stood on the second step. I moved my head very slightly to the side and there she was: my mother. She'd managed to open the front door. She was now in the hallway, crawling on the floor towards the stairs. I felt so ashamed of her. *Why is she even alive?* I thought. He's gone, and yet she's still here. It's not right.

I waited for ages to go inside. The sun had started to dip behind the houses, so I knew I'd been there for a good bit. I sneaked in and realised that she'd somehow managed to get up the stairs, because she wasn't in any of the rooms downstairs. When I went up to her bedroom, there she was, lying across the bed. *I hope you choke*, I thought.

She orders me to make her a cheese-and-pickle sandwich. Even though she trampled over my drawings, I set the tray up nicely, in the hope that it might please her. It's funny how you never completely give up hope, I think – and besides, if I bring her tea in bed, she just might go back to sleep again. It's only late in the afternoon, and I don't want her stomping around all night.

I leave the tray beside her. She just mumbles something.

I decide that I'm not staying here this evening, because she's going to wake up and start lashing out properly in a while. I can't be here for that. Before Sean left home, ages ago, he showed me how to use the phone box in case I ever needed it. He never said why I might need it, but I know now that it was in case I was ever in real danger. I am in real danger, I know, but I don't tell my family what's happening because I feel embarrassed and scared. Embarrassed to tell them about the men in my room, and really scared in case Mammy finds out that I ratted on her. She'd probably kill me stone dead. It's easier just to wait until I can legally leave home when I'm sixteen.

I decide that I'm going to ring Linda, a friend from school, not for any particular reason – I just want to get out of this house. Besides, I like Linda's mammy, because she always makes me a nice dinner when I go over to play. I head across the road and see there's a queue out-side the phone box. There's always a poxy queue, because so many people don't have phones at home. The girl inside the booth is crying, then shouting. I reckon she's splitting up with her boyfriend. There's a big gap under the door, and you can hear everything.

Some people in the queue start giggling to each other. I feel sorry for her, but when she's been in there for ages, I'm not feeling sorry for her any more: I'm just getting cold. The first person in the queue kicks the door and says, 'For fuck's sake, are you going to split up with him or not? We haven't got all day.'

When it's my turn, I suddenly feel all grown up. My very first phone call. I put the money in the slot and wait for it to drop. I love the clicking sound the phone makes each time you turn the dial with your fingers. I'm hoping I've dialled the right numbers, because I don't have much change. Linda's mammy answers the phone and immediately invites me up for tea. What more could I ask for? A safe place and some hot food. Linda's mammy doesn't ever ask me about my mammy, but I think she knows what's going on. When Daddy was alive, the guards were often called to our house, and because Linda's aunt lives only across from us, she would have told Linda's mammy.

Lately, with all the things that Mammy is doing, I'm doubting there's a God, but I do believe there's something up there that makes goodness. I look at every sunset as a sign from above. I watch it every day, and it gives me such peace. When I get home, I run out the back, grab my bike and bring it through the hall and out the front. I hop on it, and off I head for the laneway leading to Murph's field. I need to be as quick as I can, so I can get there before heading to Linda's. I just about make it. I pull on the brakes and put one foot on the ground. It's so quiet, and there's no one else around. I gaze at the last of the sun disappearing. Watching this each day keeps me going to the next one.

CHAPTER TWENTY

GROWING UP AT LAST

'M THIRTEEN YEARS OLD NOW, but womanhood is a strange concept for me, because I've always felt a lot older than I am. Even as a small child, I felt old. Now, however, things are starting to grow, and it scares me a little. *How will they know when to stop growing?* I wonder. I also have hair under my arms and on my groin. This, I really don't like. I'd love to have a moustache, though. Those stick-on ones that I wear for dressing up are a pain in the ass.

I got my period for the first time a few months ago. I didn't tell Mammy, so I had no idea how I was going to manage it. The bleeding didn't bother me at all, and I'm very lucky because I can almost guess what day it's going to start. I don't get cramps and I'm no more cranky than usual. But at first, I had no idea about pads or tampons or anything. I know that Clare used them, of course, but

I never knew exactly how. I'm just too embarrassed to ask any of my sisters.

I went down to a supermarket where no one knew me and where I could spend ages in the toiletry section, trying to figure out how exactly all these things worked without feeling mortified. *Oh, my God*, I said to myself. *Why do there have to be so many different sanitary towels?* Some are so thick, too. They'd be okay when I'm wearing my school uniform skirt, but how would I manage in trousers? I bought a few different packs, and I thought that I could try them all out. I needed to be careful that Mammy didn't find out, though, because she would just start taunting me over it. I hate when she humiliates me. It's the same with my chest. I need to start wearing a bra, but I've no idea how to go about it. Yeah, of course I know where I can get them, but how will I know which size to buy? How does anyone know? I'd be too mortified to ask my sisters or anyone in the shop to help me. I decide that I'll wait another while, then I'm just going to have to buy one myself and hope for the best.

At least sex education was most enlightening for me. Mammy called me into the front room a while ago. She was pretty hammered, but I knew that she was nervous by her body language, which was unthreatening for once. An uncommon sight. She was sitting right in front of the Superser gas heater, and the gassy, stuffy smell filled the room. I hate it.

'I want to talk to you about something,' she began.

I knew what was coming. *This will be interesting*, I thought. I almost felt sorry for her in her embarrassment. Then I kind of revelled in it as well. She looked small and almost scared. She was holding a little battered book in her hand, and as I sat, she cast her gaze towards the Superser and started to tell me about 'the birds and the bees', as she called it. At the end of her speech, she went silent for ages, handed me the book and said, 'Don't let anyone touch you down there.' I knew where she was talking about. I knew exactly what she meant. I just wished she had the balls to say the word. I got my sex education a long time ago. I could tell you everything about it from first-hand experience.

Recently, myself and my mates were walking through the local park when suddenly a flasher popped out from the bushes, flapping his penis from side to side. My mates legged it, shouting and screaming, but I stood there impatiently. I had no time for this nonsense, given the environment I lived in. I looked at him and said, 'Is that it? Have you nothing better to be doing?' He skulked back into the bushes, looking very dejected. He got me on a bad day! I walked on and caught up with the rest of the gang, who were still trying to compose themselves.

When Mammy finished her short speech, I stood up and walked out with my book in my hand. My little well of information. I headed out the back and tossed it in the hedge.

I sat on the wall for a bit and thought about sex. *Well, if I do get pregnant,* I thought, *it'll be by one of her fellas.* Other than that, I doubt it's going to happen. It's certainly not something I'd imagine doing voluntarily or enjoying. I am terribly affectionate, but I just haven't had the opportunity to express my affection with anyone since Daddy died. Not on my own terms, anyway. I cast my mind back to the day when myself and the lads walked bare-chested through the cornfields. I can still feel the bristles of the corn on my chest. I savour that feeling, because I know it's something I'll never be able to do again with the lads. I'm a woman now, and I feel that all my innocence is gone.

CHAPTER TWENTY-ONE

SHAKESPEARE ON A PINT

'THE FIELDS OF ATHENRY' IS BLASTING FROM THE RADIO. Oh, God, I hate it. This music, all day and all night. I wouldn't mind so much if it wasn't so loud the whole time. She has RTÉ Radio One playing constantly in the kitchen and in her bedroom. When I get into bed, I put cotton wool in my ears to drown out some of the noise while I'm reading. I absolutely love reading now that I've got the hang of it, thanks to my teacher. It's as if I'm making up for lost time. General-knowledge books and books about the natural wonders of the world are my favourites. I love learning new things. Stamp-collecting is something I've taken up as well. One of the girls in school has a relative in Papua New Guinea, and she gives me the most amazing colourful stamps.

Now that I'm in secondary school, my world is getting bigger. Sometimes at the weekend, I get the bus up to my sister Maria to mind her children, and I stay over. Once the kids are settled, I have a gorgeous, relaxing bath; I enjoy floating in the hot water without being afraid that Mammy will crash in and comment on what she sees. Maria always looks after me, making me a big fry-up for breakfast the next day. It's a real safe haven and a great break from the carry-on at home.

Because I'm so glad to be out, I don't say much about Mammy while I'm with my sister, but it's just lovely not to be looking over my shoulder all the time. Sometimes I wonder if any of them know what Mammy's like now and how bad it's become at home. I think they must do, because one evening, recently, my brother Sean called in unexpectedly and asked me if I wanted to go out for a bit. I was so excited. We headed for the bus stop and got the bus to town. He told me to go into any clothes shop I wanted and pick out an outfit. I couldn't believe it: I'd never had the chance to pick out my own clothes before. I got a pair of jeans and a T-shirt. I love them. He then brought me for a burger and chips. I will never forget that day. Still, I don't know why, but I don't tell my siblings about the madness that goes on in the house. I reckon there isn't much anyone can do about it, anyway.

One place of refuge is the stables near the Phoenix Park, and every now and then, I go horse riding – it depends on how much money I have from doing jobs. I love the freedom of sitting on the horse, listening to the wind in the trees, watching the deer eat the grass. I don't have any riding gear except an old riding hat. To stop the inside of my knees from rubbing against the saddle, I wear tights inside my jeans. Someone gave me this tip a while ago, and I couldn't believe it worked.

I love going for a canter in the park: it reminds me of watching *Black Beauty* on a Sunday afternoon when I was a kid. I did have a big scare one Sunday, though. The horse that was behind me came too close to mine, and my horse bucked and took off at a full gallop. Initially I loved it, feeling the wind rushing past my ears as he galloped along. But then my logic took over, along with the certainty that I'd fall off and be injured. I started to panic. I lost control of the horse, the reins and the stirrups. I quickly realised that if I didn't do something soon, I would be in big trouble. I just clung on to the horse's neck, but the movements he made were too forceful for me, and I started to get really tired. I then slid out of the saddle altogether but didn't let go. He was going so fast, and I was desperately trying to figure out how I could jump off safely. In the meantime, one of the instructors had galloped up alongside me, shouting directions. It was just white noise: I could only concentrate on what I was doing. Before long, my whole body slid right around the horse's neck. By that stage, I was clinging on for dear life while looking up at his face. I don't know why or how, but just before we got to the road, he did a big circle, slowed and stopped. I dropped off and immediately said I was fine, gasping for breath. This was partly out of embarrassment, but also to reassure them. I didn't want any fuss.

The second leader came up and ordered me to get straight back on the horse. This, I thought, was a little cruel, but I followed the order. The leader then stayed with me as we just walked our horses for the rest of the session. When the rest of the group went off for a trot, the leader explained that if I hadn't got straight back on that horse, it was unlikely that I would ever get on one again. I'm so glad now they made me do it. My arms were sore for about two weeks after that.

The one hobby that has taken a back seat is my drawing. Since I had my little exhibition, I haven't drawn anything. I will get back to it, I think. I just find it hard to escape into my drawings these days. It's as if a tiny little piece of me died that day when Mammy walked all over them. It's hard to describe, but I feel that I'm not as spontaneous these days and prefer my own company. I still see my friends, but I don't feel like hanging around as much. Music is something I'm really into now. I just love Madness, Eurythmics, Alison Moyet, The Communards and Elton John. I stick on the headphones and spend hours in front of the mirror, pretending I'm a singer. It takes me away from everything that's happening around me and reminds me of dressing up in Daddy's tails all those years ago.

Mammy has started to stay up really late at night now, muttering and playing the radio at full blast. One night, it was two o'clock in the morning, and she was still going on downstairs. I'd lie there and think, *Just three more years until I'm sixteen and old enough to leave home and get a job and a place of my own.* I don't even know if I can hang on until then. It's funny, because on the one hand, I enjoy my life: reading, listening to music, horse riding... I feel that I'm really living it; but on the other, thoughts of killing myself are never far away. Sometimes, I can be reading, and the thought will suddenly come into my head. Before, I always used to think that if I didn't make it, it would be because she killed me, but these days, I've begun to think seriously of killing myself again. Mammy's behaviour is starting to wear me down, and I feel like I don't have the energy to fight her any more.

After my confirmation, I went into a pound shop with her and I bought myself a little pen knife. I love it. It has a green handle and two blades, one long and one short. I ran it gently over my wrists one night, breaking the skin, but didn't have the nerve to go any further. The temptation occupies my mind a lot these days, but then I remember that people are looking out for me. My brothers and sisters, my friends, the teacher who helped me to catch up with my learning and who constantly encouraged me during those few weeks of human interaction in primary school. Her kindness and unconditional care gave me faith in human nature, and memories of our sessions always pull me back from the edge.

Sometimes, I look at my fingertips and remind myself that no two people have the same fingerprint. Each human being is an individual. We have our own identity. I am not like anyone else, and no one else is like me. Again, I vow to hold on for another bit.

It's hard, though, because each time I think that Mammy is quietening down a bit, she comes up with a new game. She took one up a few weeks ago: after she gets in from the pub, she goes up and down the landing reciting lines from Shakespeare. One night, at about two or three o'clock in the morning, she was ranting away, and I yelled, 'Will you go to bed!' I had an exam the next day – not that she knew anything about it. Silence. Then the Shakespeare intensified, getting louder and louder. I wrapped my arms around my head and brought my knees up to my chest, as if to make myself small and disappear altogether. Then, the door swung open with a bang, and in she came, a glass of water in her hand. 'Oh, to sleep, perchance to dream, whether 'tis nobler in the mind to suffer the slings and arrows of outrageous fortune...' The lines from *Hamlet* were all mixed up, but in a way, I was surprised that she knew them so well. Then she walked over to the bed and slowly poured a pint of water right over me.

As she exited, she turned and said, 'If you make one move in that bed, you're fucking dead.'

I lay there and accepted the situation. If I moved to get up and put on dry pyjamas, she'd hear the bed creak and she'd come in and beat me, so I just succumbed. I got up the minute the sun rose the next morning and got ready for school. I could hear her snoring through the wall. I was the first person to arrive for assembly.

CHAPTER TWENTY-TWO

I'LL JUMP

IN SCHOOL TODAY, we were talking about Shakespeare. I was able to quote a few lines from his plays, and the teacher seemed a bit surprised. It's my little secret! I'm also obsessed with history, both Irish and European. I can't get enough of the War of Independence and the Civil War, or World War II, and I soak up any information that I can find on these subjects. When I do my homework, I write each paragraph in my notes in a different colour. It helps me to keep motivated. A paragraph in red ink can't be written without being followed up by one in blue, then a green one and so on. It's just like the little pebbles in the laneway that I felt responsible for when I was a kid. I feel that everything I encounter – be it a creature or an inanimate object or a piece of information – has a little pulse to it, a soul, and I need to keep it in order. Someone said recently, joking, that I had obsessive compulsive disorder. I just laughed it off.

In spite of my extra lessons in primary school, I still struggle with learning. Sometimes, when the teachers show us videos, I can understand easily, but when the teacher talks about something, it just doesn't make sense in my head. I can only ever manage to get Cs or Ds at my best, even though I try so hard. Mammy constantly says I'm stupid and thick, but I so want to prove her wrong. Actually, it's not her I want to prove it to: it's me. I deserve to give myself the best shot. I'll just keep trying and trying. It's funny, but when I hear teachers calling my name, it makes me feel really proud. I love to hear my name being said out loud like that, as if I'm a real person. Mammy never calls me by my name. She refers to me as 'you'. She calls the new dog by its name but can't manage to do it with me. That's why, when I hear my name being said out loud, it makes me feel equal to everyone else.

What helps me to learn better are the images I see in the books and videos. The subject makes more sense to me, then. I'm a visual learner. For example, Mammy bought herself an electric drill a while ago. When she tried to explain to me how it worked, it made no sense, but when she demonstrated it, I could understand exactly. I'm a quick learner when it comes to something like DIY and only need to be shown once before I get the hang of it. It's a funny thing, but the only time Mammy isn't aggressive with me is when she's showing me how to use tools. I don't know why this is – maybe because I'm good at practical things. I appreciate her doing this, and I think it makes her feel good too.

I'm fifteen and in third year now, and in school I look out for the younger kids and chat to some of the ones who are on their own. Starting a new school can be scary at the best of times. I remember looking out the window in sixth class and seeing the secondary school across the fields. It filled me with dread. The unknown seemed so frightening at the time. Now, each day, I walk the short-cut home from school through Murph's land. Well, actually, it's not Murph's land any more, it's just loads of newly built housing estates. I reminisce about all of us collecting the scraps of wood for our bonfires and camps when it was a building site.

One day, when I get to the house, I open the door and I immediately smell gas. I drop my bag on the floor in the front room and head for the kitchen to turn the gas off for the millionth time. However, as I walk through the door, I see that the gas hasn't been left on by accident. This time, she's playing out one of her little scenes. She's always doing stuff like this now. She seems to enjoy being dramatic – all the more because I know that she has no intention of going through with her threats to kill herself. I'm not sure what she's looking for when she does this, but I'm not going to give it to her.

Now, she's on her knees, with her head in the oven. When she realises that I'm in the kitchen, she starts wailing and crying. 'I'm going to end it all, I can't do it any more.'

I just step over her feet, get a glass of milk and head upstairs. *For God's sake*, I think. I have an exam tomorrow. I want to give it my best shot.

I sit on the end of the bed, gazing out at the traffic, the way Daddy used to. I moved into this bedroom after he died, and it feels like yesterday when all that happened, even though it's been five years. I have a pencil drawing of a horse that he did for me years ago, and I treasure it. I have to hide it very carefully from her, though, ever since she got into my diary. I'd been writing in it for the previous couple of years. It wasn't so much events that I wrote about: it was more about my feelings. Those feelings were very personal, and it was the only way I had to express them. I used to be able to lock the diary with a little key, but Mammy broke it open. So now she knows my innermost thoughts and how I feel about her. I can't do anything about that, but I need to find another way of managing my thoughts, a way that she can't find out about.

I wouldn't really get into anything deep like that with my friends, even though they're dead on. I just like to have a bit of craic with them. Being with them is an escape. Anyway, it might be kind of hard for my friends to relate to what's going on in my house. Anytime I go to their houses, their families seem friendly to each other. The atmosphere in their houses seems safe. They don't shout at each other, and I never sense any aggression. It's a little unnerving. I nearly prefer my own house, because at least I know what I'm dealing with. It all really confuses me. I just don't know what's normal and what's not normal. But I do know what's right and what's wrong.

I realise now that I'm too distracted to study. *Okay, that's it. I need to get out of here. I'll study later*, I say to myself. I go downstairs to the kitchen. Mammy storms past me and thumps up the stairs. As I stick on my jacket, I hear her going into my room. I don't care. There's nothing private in there any more. The sanitary towels and Daddy's drawing, I keep in my schoolbag. It's the one place she'd have no interest in.

As I close the front door behind me, I hear her shouting over my head. I ignore it, but when I get to the gate, I turn around to find that she has climbed out of my window and is now standing on the ledge over the porch.

'If you leave, I'll jump,' she screams.

'Fuck this,' I mutter to myself. She's done this loads of times, now, threatening to kill herself if I leave, and I keep going back. I'm not doing it any more.

I get past the neighbour's house when she screams again, 'I swear, I'll jump!'

I lose my patience now. I swing around and say: 'Well, just do it then and stop going on about it!' I take a chance and turn around again. I don't look back.

CHAPTER TWENTY-THREE

THE GREAT ESCAPE

O F COURSE, I DID GO BACK. I walked around and around the block vowing never to return, but at the thought of where I might go, I got scared. Now that I can leave without getting into trouble with the law, I just don't know how to. Turning my life in a whole new direction fills me with dread. I've only just done my Inter Cert before the summer holidays and turned sixteen in July. A couple of hours later, I let myself in the back door. Mammy was sitting beside the Superser, reading. She looked up at me and then returned to her book, as if what had happened earlier was just a dream.

Mammy's told me to get a part-time job because she wants me to start paying her rent. By the weekend I have a job in a supermarket. During the school term, I work Thursday evenings, Friday evenings and all day Saturdays, so that I can make as much money as possible and save it up for my escape. It turns out that I really love the independence of working and earning my own money. On Thursday and Friday evenings, I walk straight up after school, and even though it takes me about an hour, I don't mind the walk. It clears my head. I work at the checkouts, mostly. My colleagues would be on the till, and I'd stand behind them packing bags. Depending on who I'm partnered with, we can have some fantastic conversations and a good bit of craic as well. At the end of the night, it's my job to clean my station and get it ready for the next day. I take a lot of pride in the way I pack people's groceries. You do get the odd customer who just shoves everything in any old way. At the start, I used to advise them about the correct bag-packing procedure, which of course they didn't appreciate, so now, when they impatiently fling eggs in with Parozone, I just think to myself, *Go for it!*

Ella is my favourite cashier. She calls me Mario, because she says I'm the spit of a Spanish waiter she knows. I'm pretty flattered, I must say. If I'm partnered with someone else, Ella always tries to poach me. She's very attractive, and I feel quite drawn to her. I'm a bit confused, because I thought I liked boys. The packers, like me, wear the supermarket sweaters, which are not one bit appealing. They're just shapeless things. The girls on the tills all look lovely and smart in their fitted uniforms. I don't mind the jumper so much when I'm packing, but if I'm doing stock-taking or collecting the trolleys from the car park, I feel really self-conscious, as I've put on an awful lot of weight, and I hate how I look at the moment. I look blown up, as if I'm on steroids or something, and my legs are so fat. In school, I manage to hide it to a degree by sitting behind the desk as much as I can, even at lunch break. I wear a long coat that covers a multitude of sins, and this gets me in and out of school. I also wear it walking up to work.

I eat whenever I get a chance. It doesn't matter what it is. I even eat things that I don't like. There was a tin of cocoa in the house the other day, and I just had the whole lot of it. I make my own dinner most evenings, but it's usually fried eggs and chips or spice burgers or really cheap hamburgers. They're only 10 pence each. Mammy buys loads of them. I eat lots of bread as well, and I'm addicted to cheese and milk. I have a double chin, and I just feel shit. When I walk to work, my inner thighs chafe against each other and blister during the hot weather. St Patrick's Day was particularly humiliating. The supermarket had a float in the parade. There were the tillers, the butchers, the bakers and all the rest of us staff. We had to perform a roaring 1920s dance piece. I was mortified beyond belief, parading around, all five foot and thirteen stone of me, in an oversized blue sweater and white pants, dancing in the pissing rain down O'Connell Street for the whole nation to witness. Well, if that doesn't take you out of yourself, I don't know what does.

*

The end with Mammy, when it comes, takes me by surprise. It begins when I decide to have a relaxing bath, just after Mammy leaves for the pub. I ease myself into the water and slowly sit back. I take a deep breath and place a cloth over my chest. There's a fly on the ceiling, and I don't want him gawking at me. I know that it sounds silly, but I'm very self-conscious.

As I close my eyes and think back on the day, the door bursts open. *Jesus!* I sit up frantically. Mammy is standing in front of me, screaming at me for using the hot water and the electricity. She then runs her eyes the full length of my body, which is now quite short, as my legs automatically folded up to try and conceal my groin. I press the cloth against my chest, but it doesn't cover everything. 'What have you got to hide, anyway?' she says, as she roughly pulls the cloth away. She walks out laughing. I sit in the bath until the water is cold. I'm just praying she's asleep at that stage. I can't chance it any sooner, and I've been violated enough for one day. I was so sure it was safe, even though there's no key in the bathroom door, and she's taken off the handle as well. The cold has got under my skin, and I shiver uncontrollably as I ease myself in slow motion out of the bath. I dry myself and as I'm putting my head through my pyjama top, I look at that fly on the ceiling and think, *You lucky bastard, you can just fly away.* I'll empty the water tomorrow. The noise will only wake her.

The rest of the week is mercifully quiet, until Saturday. I'm walking home from my shift, dreaming of soaking my feet. They are so tired and sore from standing in the one spot all day. Someone gave Mammy a foot spa as a present, and I use it now and then, but only when she's not in. I turn the key in the front door, hoping that she won't be there and I can borrow it, but just as I lift my first foot into the hall, she suddenly appears out of nowhere and tells me to leave again. She plants her two feet solidly on the floor and tells me, 'You're not welcome in my house any more.'

I try to brush past her to go to my room, so she can rant all she wants downstairs and I don't have to listen, but she shoves me back towards the front door. She's like a sack of spuds. Her weight is dense and strong. She glares right in my eye, a look full of sheer hatred. She then raises her right arm slowly and tightens her fist in preparation to hit me.

The decision has been made for me. I manage to block her fist with my arm as she slams towards me. I blank out. When my awareness comes back, I'm shocked to see that both of my hands are clenched tightly around her throat. Time now has a different dimension. I can't feel my body. I'm outside of it, feeling nothing. My awareness moves in waves. It comes in again, and now her face is purple. I hear faint screaming, as if from a distance. Suddenly, I come to and release my hands. She stands there, motionless. I think to myself, *That's how I used to look*. It's interesting to see that expression on someone else's face.

She very slowly steps back, and I just walk on up the stairs, as if nothing has happened. But something did happen: I felt a power in me I'd never felt before, and not in a good way. I now realise my capability, and it frightens me. How simple it would have been to kill her. But it would solve nothing. She'd be dead, and I'd be locked up.

There's only one answer. I know that I need to try and put an escape plan in place, but how do I know it's going to work when everything in this house is so unpredictable? I think about last year, when I completely shut down for a bit – I just stopped communicating with everyone – and my siblings arranged for me to join a group for the children of alcoholics. There's a centre not too far from the house. After a few sessions, it became apparent that I was the only one in the group who didn't open up or get emotional. I was then advised to join the adult group. The same thing happened there. The facilitator took me aside and told me very simply that it was my choice – I could participate in the sessions or not – and that in this life, I could sink or swim.

At the time, I thought to myself, *Well, you're a hard bitch*, but then those words made complete sense to me. I think of the day on the beach when Daddy decided to teach me how to swim. I had no choice then but to sink or swim, and my natural instinct was to survive. We all have that instinct. From the time we scavenged and lived in caves, facing danger after danger, we managed to pull through.

After a few sessions at the addiction centre, I started to think about Mammy in a different way. I now realised that what I did made absolutely no difference to Mammy's behaviour. I was no longer in her orbit, but instead, I imagined that I was on the outside looking in. When I stepped back, I understood that there are actually qualities about her that I admire. She seems to be really good at managing money. She's forever putting money in and out of various savings bonds or certificates. When she gets the bills in the post, she pays them promptly. She never takes out loans and waits until she has the money saved up before buying something. She's very thrifty, which, of course, that generation would have been anyway. She's extremely industrious and independent, which I admire. I'd like to think I have the same kind of work ethic that she has.

Mammy is really good at practical things, too. She looks after the garden, cutting the hedge with a hand shears. She has always painted the outside of the house and the garden wall herself, and she paints and decorates the inside, too. She's brilliant at general DIY. I've learned a lot of practical skills from Mammy, just by watching her. She's changed plugs, measured walls, drilled holes, hung pictures and papered walls. She's even taught me how to change a glass windowpane. On numerous occasions, when she couldn't find her house keys to get in at night, she would smash the small window in the front room to get her arm in and open the bigger window, so she could climb in. Sometimes I wouldn't hear her because I'd have my headphones on. The next day, she'd send me down to the hardware shop to get a bag of putty and a piece of glass to replace the window. I love replacing the window myself. It makes me feel really grown up. I also love the smell of the putty and the feel of it as I'm pressing it securely around the frame.

My experience in the addiction centre made me realise, though, that I can't stay in my house much longer. Whatever I do, I want to finish school. Even if I do badly in my exams, it's something she can't take away from me. Home scares the life out of me, but as bad as this existence is, it's all I know. I feel so tired the whole time now. I don't express much verbally with anyone these days. I just don't see the point. I looked at all my little bits and pieces in the room recently and realised that I own very little: a bike and a hairdryer. My drawings, I keep in my room now. Time seems to go so differently in this house. Sometimes I feel like I'm stuck in time. I've become quiet to the point where I hardly speak at all. The fear of killing her is very real. I want her out of my life, but I know that I don't want her blood on my hands. I need to find every ounce of strength

I have to rise above that. I want freedom and I want a future.

I spend endless nights fretting about leaving, even though I know I have no choice. I try to figure out how I'll know when the time is right. Is it a case that someday soon I'll just pack a few bits, say 'I'm going' and walk out the front door? Or maybe I'll pack my stuff one night and leave before she comes home from the pub. Thinking about it really upsets and distresses me. At the moment, the fear of leaving seems to be worse than the situation itself. Then I think of Daddy. He was weak and unable to fight Mammy, but his swimming lessons showed me that he wasn't afraid to take a chance. This gives me a little courage. I guess I have nothing to lose.

It's a Thursday evening, a few days after I attacked Mammy. I'm just inside the front door when she flies out of the kitchen and launches an onslaught of verbal abuse at me. It's the usual mantra: 'You're nothing, you're a worthless piece of shit, I should have drowned you at birth.' My body takes me upstairs, all the time aware that she's not too far behind me. My hand reaches for my underwear drawer, and I pull out whatever I can manage and stuff it down my shirt. I grab my drawings, all the while hearing a torrent of abuse in the background. None of the words sting any more, and I'm just not willing to physically hurt another human being. I have too much respect for myself, and my dignity is too important to me. Her screaming sounds just like her radio: not so much intimidating any more, just annoying.

I open my bedroom window and throw my drawings down on to the ground. They give a big thud, and as I look down, I think, *Jesus Christ, I'm going to die!* But at the same time, I can't go back in there. I grab the window frame and ease myself out on to the windowsill. I see the ground below me and I just feel sick. I then kneel on my window ledge and lower my legs outside slowly, until I can feel the ledge over the porch under my feet. My hands are still gripping the edge of my bedroom window. The next thing, Mammy appears, beating my fingers with her fists while screaming obscenities at me. Again, she screams, 'I should have drowned you at birth.'

Even though I'm now standing on the ledge above the porch, I'm blinded by temper. I reach in, grab her by the throat and shout, 'Well, why the fuck didn't you, then?' while pushing her off me. Afraid of what I might do if I don't leave now, I lower my knees carefully on to the ledge and start to ease my body over, feet first. If I land badly, I'm acutely aware that I could just split my skull and die. I'm now dangling in mid-air. For a split second, I think, *Why didn't I throw my blankets out first, for a softer landing?* But I just didn't have the time. My body loses its grip, and I fall. I land right on my hip. My adrenaline is pumping, and I get up straight away. I grab my bundle of drawings. I'm now delirious. I head for the main road. It's really busy with traffic, but I make it across.

I'm limping badly now, but I don't feel anything. I hear a truck blowing its horn behind me. I look around to see Mammy standing in the middle of the road. I don't believe this. The truck missed her by about an inch. I'm so disappointed that it didn't hit her. I can't believe she's coming after me. I start to run now from bus stop to bus stop. Eventually, a bus comes, and I manage to hop on. As I walk towards the end of the bus, I can still see her charging up the road. I collapse on to a seat. I now start to shiver uncontrollably. The enormity of what just happened is shocking for me. Never, ever, in my wildest dreams, did I think I'd be leaving home that way.

I have no idea where I'm going. I decide to go to Clare's, and without even noticing the journey, I'm at her door. I don't have to say anything: she takes me in immediately, no questions asked. *I'll explain everything to her tomorrow*, I think. I soon pass out with exhaustion.

PART THREE

A CERTAIN FREEDOM

CHAPTER TWENTY-FOUR

THE LAST MEETING

I T'S NOW 1988, and I've been living with my sister Clare for some months. I haven't seen or heard anything from Mammy since I left home. Since that night, there's been an ominous silence from her, and sometimes I almost feel that I miss her. Even though she's nearly destroyed me, she's still the only home I've ever known. I don't feel completely free because I'm expecting her to call up any day and demand that I go back home to her, even though I am now seventeen and legally not obliged to. Those old feelings of fear and intimidation creep in on me every now and then.

Then, out of the blue, she rings Clare and demands that I speak to her on the phone. Initially, I think I'll just ignore her, but then I'm curious. I mean, she can hardly hurt me down a phone line.

When I take the handset in my hand, I raise it to my ear but say nothing.

'Are you there?' Mammy says. 'Are you there?'

Nothing.

On the third attempt she says, 'Aisling, are you there?' quite aggressively.

Wow, I think. *She said my name.* 'Yes.'

'Are you coming home?'

'No.'

'This is ridiculous. At least come down and see me.'

I wonder if this is a trap. I say, 'I don't know.'

'What kind of an answer is that?' she says.

I go silent again. After a very long pause, she says she'll ring me back again the next day. I put the handset down. I feel really shaky after it. That whole night I can't sleep with anxiety. Is she just going to keep harassing me now, even though I've left home?

True to her word, she does ring me the next day. At the end of the conversation, which is quite short, she says, 'I beg you to come down and see me.' She seems desperate, but I know I have to be cautious. I don't want to get pulled back into her web again.

I hear myself say, 'Okay.' It doesn't even enter my head to say I'll meet her in a public place, like a cafe. It just so happens that the final parent–teacher meeting is on the Friday of that week. Mammy has never been to any of the parent–teacher meetings in secondary school. That used to really upset me. Now I tell Mammy about it and I add, 'Would you go to the parent–teacher meeting, and I can see you in the house after? I might even stay over.'

She agrees, and I get so excited. *Oh, my God*, I think, *this is a great idea.* I so want her to meet my teachers. I want her to hear with her own ears what they have to say about me, because I've always got good school reports and I've never been in trouble. I've never been cheeky or answered back. Whenever I witnessed the odd kid being smart to the teacher, I used to be tempted to tell them to just grow up.

I have never been academically minded, as you know, and I have to work really hard for the grades I get. When I hear schoolmates cribbing that they only got a C when they were expecting a B, I roll my eyes. In the subjects I enjoy, Cs and Ds are my best grades, and I am over the moon with that. I keep all my school reports in a little tin box, savouring all the complimentary comments, like, 'Tries her best', 'Polite', 'A pleasure to teach'. I feel so proud of these comments because they're so personal. These little slips of paper with my name on the top are actually about me. Mammy has never asked for my reports, so I've never shown them to her. She doesn't know what subjects I'm doing or what teachers I have.

A while ago, my art teacher asked me to stay back after school. I knew I wasn't in trouble, so I wasn't anxious. She said that two people had been shortlisted for the school art award: myself and another classmate. In the end, she chose me because she said I seemed to put more work in. I couldn't believe I was hearing this. I was presented with the most beautiful hardback book with my name inscribed in calligraphy on the inside cover. When I ran home after school, I left it on the kitchen counter, hoping Mammy would notice it and comment. If I showed it to her myself, I would be ridiculed. When I came down to the kitchen that evening, the book was on the floor. I picked it up gently and brought it upstairs quietly.

Now I'm hoping for better. It's Friday, and I pack a little bag: socks, jocks, a fresh top and a little bag with a toothbrush and some deodorant in it. As I walk towards Mammy's, I feel nervous and excited at the same time. When I get to the house, I don't quite know what to do. Do I ring the doorbell or just open the door with my key? I ring the doorbell. I'd give anything to try and salvage something from this wreck of a relationship, not that we ever really had one in the first place. I've never given up hope, though.

After ringing the doorbell three times, I have no option but to use my key. The first thing that hits me is the smell, a stale, stagnant one. They say each house has its own smell; I had forgotten what ours was like. There is a deathly silence as I walk in, and I know immediately that she's not in, because I don't sense her presence. In my innocence, I convince myself that she's just gone to the shop. It's midday now, and the parent–teacher meeting isn't until six o'clock this evening, but I have a grinding feeling in my stomach that she's gone to the pub to see her drinking buddies. Part of me is hoping she doesn't go to the meeting now. I then give her the benefit of the doubt. Maybe she's had to go into town to pay some bills and is heading to the meeting straight after.

It's now half past eleven at night, and I've been hanging around here all evening. Why did I stay? It's too late now to get a bus back to Clare's. It's as if the house put a spell on me or something. The door eventually bangs open. I look over the banisters and see a man helping Mammy in. She's practically dragging her feet, her arms slung over his shoulder. The two of them collapse on the stairs.

I retreat back into my room. I pray that he stays, so I won't have to deal with her. Then I suddenly feel like I want to get the vase from the landing and smash it over the guy's head. I remember when Mammy threw Daddy down the stairs years ago and threatened to throw a vase at me when I ran down to help him. Nothing has changed, absolutely nothing. I just don't know how I feel. Fooled, disgusted and deflated. I sit on my bed all night and wait till the morning.

By eight o'clock the next morning I make a move. I sneak past her bedroom but am betrayed by the creaking floorboard. 'Who's that?' she slurs from her bedroom. I bet she didn't even remember I was staying the night.

I step inside her room. She's in a bad state, her hair on end, her clothes dishevelled, even though she's wearing her fur coat. I think to myself, *You're a disgrace.* And because I've nothing to lose now, I ask her, 'How was the parent–teacher meeting?'

She incoherently says, 'Huh, well, what do you expect me to say? That I found out you're some kind of a genius?'

I don't reply. I just walk out of that house telling myself that it's for the very last time. I have no idea if she really went to the parent–teacher meeting, but I don't know if I care any more.

On Monday morning, I'm in art class, getting my stuff out of the press, and one of the nuns pulls me aside and says, 'You never told us anything about your mother.'

Oh… So, now I know: she did go, and not only that, but she went pissed.

I grit my teeth and say, 'No, Sister, I didn't tell you because if I ever got into trouble in school, I wanted to take full responsibility for myself. I didn't want my mother's behaviour to be used as an excuse for my behaviour.' I have such a sense of respect for myself. I'm not going to let my mother tar me. I want to show the nun just how sensible and mature I am, unlike Mammy.

The nun nods her head in acknowledgement. I'm really not in the mood for a chat, and I don't want to be probed any further, so I ask if I can go back to my desk. I do not want to be disrespectful, as I always take pride in how I conduct myself with people, probably because of Mammy. But as the class starts, I find myself going into some kind of a trance. This hasn't happened to me in a while. I keep thinking that what Mammy did was the ultimate betrayal. She contacted me numerous times, begging me to come down. I asked her to do just one thing, to go to the last parent–teacher meeting, and she agreed, then she turned up drunk. I feel so stupid. I had this image in my head: I'd see her before the meeting, sober, and then, after she'd come back from the meeting, we'd maybe have a chat, I'd stay overnight... maybe I'd even bring her up some brekkie the next morning. How stupid was I? At this moment, I feel dejected and lonely, then I get annoyed at myself for feeling like this. *It's sink or swim, Ais*, I tell myself. I've become quite hardened these days.

CHAPTER TWENTY-FIVE

PRESS REPEAT

REVISING FOR THE LEAVING CERT HAS BECOME A REAL STRUGGLE OVER THE LAST FEW MONTHS. After that last incident with Mammy, I seem to have lost all sense of everything. I can't even say I'm unhappy: I just feel nothing. Each night I attempt to study, but I can't relax enough. I keep checking things over and over, and by the time I get to seriously knuckling down, it's bedtime. It's not that I'm wasting time, it's just that my head is in a kind of fog, so I can't make a study plan or structure anything. I actually do feel thick. God, maybe, just maybe, Mammy was right all along. Am I fooling myself into believing I'm better than I really am?

The exams come and go. I go in and sit them all. I keep writing, even though I don't understand a lot of what I am writing. For my oral Irish exam, when I enter the room, I tell the examiner straight off that I can't speak any Irish and can't understand any of it either.

She looks at me in disbelief. 'You'll have to say something,' she says. 'I'll point to the window and the door, and if you can just say what they are in Irish, at least there'll be proof that you were here.'

'*Fuinneóg, doras,*' I say. Well, that is the end of that. I know that I've made a mess of the exams, but I'm so relieved that they're over.

The day after my final exam in school, I get a job in a diner in Dublin city. I love it. I know a couple of the girls who work there already, and the work brings me out of myself a bit. I start to laugh again. I work six days a week, Monday to Saturday, twelve noon until seven in the evening. It takes me two hours to walk to work in the morning, and I enjoy it. It clears my mind. I'm working, I am paying for my keep and I want to have some savings as well.

The pay isn't great, but it's an Italian family business, and they are lovely to work for. It's a lively spot. There's a travel agent right next door and a national newspaper publisher across the road, which brings in a lot of customers. When we are expecting a coachload of tourists, we set ourselves up like a military operation. Even so, there are two chefs, the lady on the till and just three of us on the floor for up to 160 customers. At the end of a busy run, we're all so proud to have got through it and give each other high fives. I love the teamwork. At the weekend, myself and the girls go out for a few pints and have a laugh, and even though I know that this isn't my 'forever' job, it's just what I need.

The results come before I know it. I have already decided I'm going to give art college a go, but of course that all depends on how I got on in the exams. The morning the results are due, I feel so nervous. I walk the long way up to the convent, along the windy avenue. As I walk in the main entrance, I notice that the cross on the gate is crooked. This small, insignificant thing agitates me. It seems like an omen.

When I get to the office, one of the nuns hands me my envelope. Her face gives nothing away.

I stay in the car park for a bit before opening it. It's devastating. The results make no sense whatsoever. I've failed a lot of the subjects, even subjects I loved, like history and English. I've passed accountancy, a subject I was rubbish at. I just can't grasp it.

I go to bed and cry, feeling very sorry for myself. When I wake a few hours later, I feel really angry with myself and tell myself to cop on. It's as if I'm split in two – one half is telling the other not to be so hard on me, but then the facilitator's voice from the addiction centre is going around in my head: 'Sink or swim.'

The next day, I waste no time. I go back down to school and ask them what I need to do to repeat. They tell me that I can't repeat there, so I approach another local school and am told the same thing. Someone then advises me to try the Christian Brothers school in James's Street. *But sure, that's a boys' school,* I think. Still, I ring them and, to my surprise, I'm invited in to meet the head Christian Brother. This is surreal.

The day of the meeting, I walk into the school and immediately recognise that 'boy' smell. It brings me back to fourth class in primary, when I was in the boys' school for a while. I feel safe and reassured by it. The Christian Brother greets me and invites me into his office. He is really friendly and tells me a bit about his school and how much the fees are to repeat. I quickly realise that I need to do a little bit more than save money on bus fares for this one, but I'm determined to go through with it.

All my mates are telling me to forget about repeating and to work, earning money so I can go out with them at the weekends and enjoy myself. I think to myself, *No, I'm doing this, I'm doing it for me.* I take myself back to the sense of pride I felt when I had those sessions with my teacher. She believed in me. The facilitator in AA wouldn't have taken me aside if she didn't give a shit either. She also believed in me. Now I believe in myself. I decide to work for the next year, full time. That way, I can save my ass off so I can repeat my Leaving Cert the following year.

In the meantime, my eldest sister, Louise, who lives in Amsterdam, gets me a surprise return ticket to visit her in the city. I can't believe it. I've never travelled anywhere on my own before, apart from my trip to Granny as a child. It's a huge adventure. My sister brings me to Anne Frank's house, which is amazing, because I read the book as a child. I see Rembrandt's *The Night Watch* in the Rijksmuseum, too. I could stand there and look at that painting for days. We also go to the Stedelijk Museum, which is the home of modern art, and it's there that I decide that I'll be a great artist, too. Seeing the paintings gives me the inspiration to keep going and to achieve my dream.

My sister has to work a couple of evenings while I'm there, but that suits me fine, as it gives me the chance to wander around and explore the bars, markets and little streets for myself. Amsterdam is like nothing I've ever experienced. One evening, I go to a cafe and as I sit down I take out a cigarette. (I started smoking a while back.) This gentleman walks past me, doesn't say a thing and just flicks his lighter and lights my cigarette. No words are exchanged. I look at him briefly, and he goes off into the night. It is almost like a scene from a film noir.

What really strikes me while I'm in Amsterdam is how quiet I am. I don't initiate chats with Louise or any of her friends. I just don't seem to have much to say. Also, my whole body image is very skewed. I go into my sister's bathroom in the mornings to get dressed, as she lives in a beautiful open-plan apartment, and I feel so self-conscious. When I come out of her bathroom, I am fully clothed, including my jacket. If I could cover myself from head to toe and leave nothing exposed, I would, and yet in another sense, I feel so free during this holiday. Perhaps it's a freedom from the familiar. I'm free of any kind of routine I have at home and from all the landmarks that are so familiar to me. It's a wonderful experience.

Louise asks me about Mammy, and I tell her some things, but not everything. I still feel too embarrassed to talk about the sexual abuse. I don't feel ready or able to talk about my experience in detail just yet. Hopefully, some day I will. I realise more than ever just how shut-down I've been over the past few years, and I long for the freedom of life as a real adult.

The year goes really quickly, and it's kind of nice not to have anything else in my head apart from work, which I enjoy. Myself and the girls have some fun nights out. For Halloween, we dress up as Vikings, with plaited wool for hair and miniature cardboard boats around our waists. The boats jut out about a metre at each end. We have a few beers and then get the bus into town. We sing 'Rock the Boat' as we try to manoeuvre our way up the stairs on the bus. The whole place bursts into laughter. Later, when we get to the nightclub, the bouncer asks me, 'How old are you?' I point at my costume and say, 'I'm a thousand years old – how old do you think I am?' taking some stray wool from my mouth. The girls look at me in astonishment, as I am usually the quietest out of the three of us. The bouncer laughs and says he can't argue with that, slaps me on the back and lets us into the club. Needless to say, the boats meet their grisly end once the dancing starts!

During that year, I begin to build a portfolio for art college and even catch the eye of some bloke. He's been coming into the diner for a few weeks. The girls have been slagging me that he fancies me, but I've just dismissed it. They must be right, though, because he asks me out the next time he comes in. We go to see *Dangerous Liaisons* with Glenn Close and John Malkovich. His name is Tom, and he's dead on. A few other fellas have asked me out on dates before, but this one is different. He seems so genuine and isn't afraid to look me right in the eye. My gut says he's a good person.

September comes round quickly enough, and I now have enough money for the repeat Leaving Cert. My first day at CBS is funny. I don't know why, but I wear a suit. When I arrive, the principal tells one of the boys to carry my bag. I'm given another tour of the school, and when I walk into my first class, all the boys stand up. They think I'm the teacher! That breaks the ice, anyway. The lads are dead on, and I'm well at home with them. Some are real sweethearts and some are rough around the edges, but I enjoy getting to know them all.

I now work in the diner on Saturdays and during the school holidays. It takes about an hour each way to cycle to school from my sister Maria's house. That's where I live now, with her family. I find this journey really tough after a while, especially in windy, wet weather. Sometimes I only get as far as the park, so I study there. I apply to a couple of art colleges and repeat my exams. I still find them tough but feel that I've given them a better shot this time. Anyway, I couldn't have studied any harder than I did.

When I open that envelope for a second time, I breathe a huge sigh of relief. I've made it.

CHAPTER TWENTY-SIX

INSANITY

FROM THIS POINT ON, life begins to take shape for me. After the long years of wishing and waiting, I'm finally on my way. I wonder what Mammy would make of me now, a potential art student with a boyfriend. My relationship with Mammy is unpredictable these days, but I still keep trying. Every weekend, I go over to help her with jobs about the house or the garden. I take it day by day. If she's too volatile, I just walk away. I've vowed not to rise to the bait any more. We've never talked about the day I left: we just picked up again almost as if it never happened. Sometimes I can feel the frustration building inside of me, the need to tell her what I really think.

Applying for art college is nerve-racking. I've always hated forms, and they ask so many questions, not to mention doing the portfolio and an interview. I've only applied to colleges that are relatively close to me, for convenience. I wouldn't be able to afford the public transport, as well as all the other expenses, for colleges further away. Before I got my results, when I told the art teacher in CBS where I was applying, she said that I was arrogant to assume I would get into one of those places, but it isn't arrogance that inspired me to apply to them – it's the fact that they are closest.

Anyway, I do get into one of my choices, but when I go for the first interview, one of the panel asks me if I'm on medication.

I'm astonished. 'Why would you think that?'

'It's because your artwork doesn't have any theme running through it,' he explains. I can't understand what they are talking about. I just paint emotions in whatever shape they take. The overall theme is out of my control. But then I wonder if he means a sense of the person behind the work and their ideas. I begin to think that maybe he has a point and that, in some way, some of my thoughts are disjointed because of the way I've been brought up. Sometimes, I wonder who I am.

My second interview panel seems a lot more open-minded, though, and happy to look at my works as just that: examples of my craft. I'm delighted to be offered a place at the college. I begin next week.

I've also left Maria's and moved into my first flat with Tom. It's an amazing feeling to have my own space: my own toilet, my own little kitchen, my own utensils, pots and pans. I've never felt worried about moving in with Tom. I just knew right from the start that he was a good person. On our very first evening in our new flat, I do, however, tell him that if he ever hits me, I'll throw him through the window. He nods and says, 'I know.' That understood, we get a Chinese takeaway.

Tom knows all about Mammy, and she likes him. I think it's because Tom has a huge appreciation of history and poetry, like she does. Mammy can relate to him, but he challenges her and doesn't let her get away with any insults. He stands up to her, and I think she respects that.

We live on the top floor of an old house. When you walk in, there is a little shower room to the right, with a toilet and a sink. Then there is a very small sitting room with a spiral staircase in it that leads up to the kitchen, and another spiral staircase that goes from the kitchen up to the bedroom. You can climb out the bedroom window on to a little rooftop and look over the city. There are also two huge windows in the bedroom, through which the light comes flooding in.

I love my little nest, and we settle in very quickly. I don't feel claustrophobic in the small space, and Tom doesn't swallow me up with his personality. He is really easy to live with. Thank God he does most of the cooking, because we would starve otherwise. Cooking has never been one of my talents. I would quite happily live on spaghetti and jars of tomato sauce 365 days of the year. Other than that, everything is very equal. We both get groceries and split the dusting, cleaning and laundry equally. The laundry facilities are shared with the other six flats, which means that we are constantly waiting to use a machine or dryer. This can be quite funny sometimes as, on hearing the final spin of someone's clothes in the washing machine, doors fly open and people charge into the little laundry room. I often get a smack in the head from the laundry door being swung open while bending down to retrieve my clothes.

It's now 1990, and I'm twenty years old. When I start art college, it is a huge shock to the system. I'm going from the restrictions of a convent school and a Christian Brothers school to a landscape that has very few rules. I find this very difficult. I loved the assembly lines, the order and the quietness in corridors that school provided. I was used to students opening doors for teachers and classes standing up when teachers walked into the room. Suddenly, I'm in a world where nobody reminds you about deadlines and people wander in and out of classes. In school, there was one secretary, but here, there seem to be loads of them.

What's more, I find the workload overwhelming. You seem to be left to your own devices to get on with it. The students themselves all seem very hip and cool, but the lack of routine is freaking me out. That, and the fact that

I can't tell the difference between the students and the tutors. Some are really arty-looking, in their woolly jumpers and casual jeans. When I'm sitting in the canteen, I can usually tell who's studying what just by looking at them. There are the business students, with their shirts and ties; the graphics students, with colourful shirts tucked into their trousers and neat hairstyles; and us, the fine art students, most of whom look homeless. I feel like the snobs in Mammy's church, working out who is who by the way they dress.

Even though I'm at art school, we study a broad range of subjects. They're all interesting, except for business studies, which I don't enjoy at all. Art history, philosophy and psychology, I just can't get enough of. I enjoy the written assignments, and I've been getting good marks in them – so far, so good. We also have painting, drawing and photography, which is deadly, because we develop our own black-and-white photographs. We do printing, graphics and three-dimensional studies: stone carving, wood carving and metalwork, which I love as well, because it's really physical. We've just learned how to weld metal. It's 'sink or swim', just as the counsellor at the addiction centre told me, and so far I'm swimming.

One day, my tutor calls me into her office. She looks a bit uncomfortable and ums and ahs before telling me that Mammy rang earlier.

I have no idea what to say. I wonder for a second if there's an emergency at home, before realising that there probably isn't. The tutor goes on to say that in fact Mammy rang numerous times this week. She seemed very reasonable on the phone but wanted to alert the staff to the fact that I was 'completely insane'. The tutor explains that obviously my mother is 'unwell', and while there was no urgency to tell me about the calls earlier in the week, now I have to know because, basically, Mammy is harassing me.

'My mother is a chronic alcoholic, and I think she's psychotic, too,' I say. I don't add that, in my opinion, she always has been.

The tutor just nods her head. I know that she doesn't expect me to elaborate further. My legs feel weak. This can't be happening. I can't believe Mammy is trying to hijack my education again. Then I feel my cheeks burn. 'If Mammy came into the room now,' I tell the tutor, 'I'd fucking kill her.' *Can't I do anything in my life without her poisoning it?* I wonder.

'Would you like to sit down?' the tutor says sympathetically.

I'm standing with my fists clenched. 'No,' I mutter. There's a desk between myself and the tutor, and I'm just hoping she doesn't come near me to try and console me.

She steps forward slightly, and I step back. I raise my arm and say, 'Don't.'

After a couple of minutes' silence, which I'm grateful for, I give a very brief overview of my life to date. It's mortifying. I feel as if I'm back in Mammy's web. 'Please ask admin not to transfer any more calls from her,' I ask the tutor.

'Of course,' she says. 'Can I do anything to help?'

I say no, because I'm used to handling Mammy on my own. I appreciate the support, but I'm doing okay, I think.

However, I've noticed that I've been feeling kind of sick the last while. It's some kind of a stomach thing. It could be as a result of the chemicals we use in the printing studio or the darkroom. I hate being cooped up in stuffy rooms at the best of times. The printing studio doesn't have a whole lot of fresh air coming through, and I don't wear a mask.

We do a lot of work with copper plates, and some of the acids would burn right through your skin. We do wear gloves, alright, but there must be a serious amount of fumes in the air all the same. The darkroom isn't much better. There are absolutely no windows in it for obvious reasons, and the developing fluid and the fix fluid smell really strong. Again, none of us wears a mask. We stay in the darkroom for about three hours at a time, and I always feel quite dizzy when I come out. *Maybe I'm just dehydrated*, I think to myself. I still feel as if I'm finding my feet and haven't really got into a proper routine yet. I'd want to find one, because it's nearly Christmas.

*

Tom and I spend Christmas with his family in his parents' house. I can't believe how lovely and relaxing it is after my experiences of Christmas at home. His family are a good bit of craic too. On St Stephen's Day, we both go to Maria's house. Her kids are running around playing with their Christmas presents, so we just about manage to ignore the fact that Mammy is there, pissed as usual. I don't even bother asking her about the calls to the college. I decide to say nothing to anyone about it and just try to put it behind me.

The following week, I feel dizzy and disorientated. Then, one night, I'm sitting up in bed and suddenly I feel really light-headed. I go to stand up and I collapse. *Maybe I've lost my balance*, I think. I go to stand up again, but again my legs just fold under me. I can't feel anything from the waist down.

I yell for Tom, who immediately rings for an ambulance. Because we live on the top floor, they have to take me down the stairs in one of those chair-like stretchers. I am mortified at creating such a fuss. I feel so sorry for the ambulance men, and I keep apologising.

When I arrive at the hospital, I am brought straight through. After some thorough testing, they tell me that I need surgery to remove my appendix and some ovarian cysts. I'm in the operating theatre that night. I've never had any type of surgery before, so it's all very new to me, but the hospital staff are nice and explain everything clearly. I even have a bit of craic with the surgical team.

I kind of like the sensation of the gas, counting from ten backwards until I reach about three then pass out. Before I know it, I can hear people calling my name. When I wake up, I feel very ill, weak and disorientated. I manage to shift myself from the trolley on which I'm lying to the bed, but it's not long before I need to go to the toilet. *How am I going to manage this?* I wonder. The clock on the wall tells me it's three o'clock in the morning, even though I've had no sense of time passing.

I call a nurse, and she tries to help me out of the bed, but I just can't move my legs. 'Never mind,' she says, disappearing and coming back with one of those big old stainless-steel bedpans. She manages to roll me on to it, and I try to balance myself on it as best I can, but it takes three attempts – and the nurse turning on all the taps in the ward bathrooms – for something to happen. It works, even though the noise of the running tap water wakes everyone else up.

The morning comes, and I feel like lead. No sooner is my breakfast tray placed in front of me than a nurse tells me I need to go straight back down to surgery. When I try to figure out what's going on, I'm told to sign another consent form. I'm now being wheeled on a trolley very quickly down the corridor. I get to the theatre entrance. As I look up some steps, I see the surgical team hastily making their way down, their white clogs clanking as they go. A picture of my First Holy Communion clogs and that awful day with Mammy and Daddy flashes in my head. The theatre doors are swung open. There's no chit-chat and certainly no craic. I'm waiting for someone to break the ice because I'm starting to panic. A razor blade is produced and one of the team starts to dry shave my pubic area. I stutter something and start to shiver uncontrollably. Some kind of silver blanket is wrapped around me.

That's the last thing I remember.

I wake up, and Tom is sitting there. It's so good to see him.

'I got an awful fright when you came back from theatre,' he says. 'The sheet over you was soaked in blood.' This alarmed the other patients, too. I am dimly aware of the drama, because soon after I came around, a doctor came and apologised for the urgency, but explained that they had no option because it was discovered that I had bleeding in the stomach, which needed urgent attention. I lift the blankets and look at all the dressings. 'Bloody hell. I'm going to look like "join the dots" when all this is over,' I say to Tom.

I ask Tom to inform Mammy that I'm in the hospital, but I very quickly regret it. A couple of days after the surgery, I am still feeling sore from all the poking about and am hooked up to a drip, but I'm in good form, relieved that I am soon going to be back on track. Then I see

Mammy walking through the ward. I think I'm going to be sick. I know immediately that she is pissed. She has that satanic scowl on her face.

She marches up to the bed. 'Look at you,' she says, loud enough that others can hear. 'There's fuck all wrong with you.'

I look at her in disbelief. I feel too weak to challenge her. The tears start to roll down my cheeks. Again, I am expressionless. I know better than to give Mammy too many signs of upset. After a few minutes, a nurse comes and tells her that I'm not well enough for visitors, which is a lie, but the nurse has good cop-on. Mammy starts insulting the nurse and shouting loudly that I have AIDS. The security man has to be called, and Mammy is escorted out. Not without a fight, of course. I just close my eyes. I feel so, so embarrassed and humiliated by her behaviour. Why does she do it? Did she even want to see me?

Throughout the remainder of my hospital stay, Mammy rings repeatedly. She just rants and talks gibberish. The nurses make excuses to shield me from her. They are fantastic, and for the first time in a long while, I feel myself relax.

It takes me some time to recover from my operation, and because I've missed a lot of college, I'm not surprised when I fail my first year. I've no option but to repeat. Besides, I know that I can do it – I've failed before and I've picked myself up again and got on with it. I work my ass off that summer, between shifts at the diner and painting murals on the side, which I've been commissioned to do, so that I can pay for my repeat year. On my second attempt at first year, I'm able to get really stuck in. I plough into it. The only thing that stresses me is that I have very little money for materials. The college provides the canvas material for painting, thank God, but I still need reams of drawing paper, developing paper for photography, paints and brushes.

One day, I come across some wallpaper that I once used for drawing and I adapt it into a notebook, cutting out A4-sized pages and stapling them together. Why not? When I'm in sculpture class, the tutor asks me where my proper notebook is. I tell him honestly that I can't afford one. I am determined not to feel embarrassed by this. The tutor says nothing and simply walks out of the class. *Okay*, I think, *so the class is on hold because of me*, but again, I'm not going to feel embarrassed.

A few minutes later, he returns with a gorgeous A4 hardback notebook and hands it to me. I simply say, 'Thank you,' graciously and smile at him. I am as happy as a pig in muck.

The following week, other members of the sculpture group arrive in with notebooks made of stapled-together bits of wallpaper, in the hope that they'll get a cool hardback one like I did. I get a great laugh out of this.

CHAPTER TWENTY-SEVEN

LEARNING TO HEAR

THE 3D SCULPTURE CLASSES ARE HELD OUTSIDE, in sheds around the yard. The yard is filled with blocks of granite in various sizes, long metal rods, which we use for welding, and large sheets of copper for hammering and shaping. These tutorials can be extremely challenging for everyone, as you might have people using angle grinders and chiselling stone at the same time, but I absolutely love the energy I get from the sculpture yard. When I have my visor and gloves on and I'm welding metal, the sparks are like stars, especially on a winter's afternoon, when it starts to get dark.

I love pummelling and cutting the copper sheets and bringing that metal hammer down on to a chisel. It always brings me back to Mammy and her meat. She should have done stone carving to relieve some of that energy! I also love using a wooden mallet for carving wood. I've learned so many new skills and feel that they will come in handy later in life. The theoretical side of 3D, I find difficult. The lingo is hard for me to understand, but I love the practical side. I just want to keep painting, chiselling, welding, moulding and carving.

The noise in the sculpture yard makes me realise that my hearing seems a little wonky the last while. When I'm in the street and there's traffic, I can't hear what people are saying, especially if they are on my left-hand side. When tinnitus kicks in and I am outdoors, it blurs out all the noise, and I am left with a very high-pitched hum in my ear, which can make me feel dizzy and nauseous. During the classes, if there are sounds like chewing or doors opening and shutting, it really throws me out of kilter. Every sound has the same level of noise for me. Often the tutor's voice is just mixed in with all of this, no matter where I sit in the room, so it's hard to hear instructions.

Eventually, I get an appointment at the Eye and Ear Hospital. The staff are lovely, and I have numerous tests, including a brain scan. It's fascinating, until they give me the results. I'm told a nerve has almost been severed in my left ear. I have lost about 70 per cent of my hearing in that ear, and I'll need a hearing aid. I will more than likely be completely deaf in that ear within five years.

I am in shock. Up until now, I haven't really taken it very seriously. I thought that it was just me being particular about sounds: I've always been used to a high level of noise, including blasting the head off myself with headphones.

I tell the guy all this, then he shows me the brain scan, with all the different layers and colours. It looks beautiful.

I nod towards the scan and say, 'Sure, look, at least I know there is something in there.' I always do this when I'm anxious. I deflect with humour.

The doctor doesn't see the funny side. I'm a bit taken aback. Why the seriousness?

A woman comes in to join us. 'Were you ever involved in a car crash?' she asks.

'No,' I say, laughing. 'Unless I was, and I forgot.'

'Oh, you'd remember this car crash,' she says. 'There is evidence here of blunt trauma to the head.'

I am just gobsmacked now.

'Do you ever remember getting a blow to the head?'

I shake my head and say, 'No,' quietly. They know I'm lying. I look at the woman, she looks at me, nods and winks. She knows.

'I think that there might be complications down the road,' the doctor says. 'Have you ever driven a car or used computers?'

'I haven't learned to drive yet, but I find using computers really hard,' I admit.

'Well, these might be things you'll struggle with in the future,' he says.

My first thought is, *Well, fuck that!* I don't care about computers, but nothing is going to stop me from learning to drive. I drove a Honda 50 motorbike up the lane when I was ten, and I had no bother with the throttle or the gears, and when I was on my pony beside Daddy in the van, I was forever watching his footwork on the pedals. Because I live in the city, I don't need a car – I couldn't afford one anyway – but when I get out to those Wicklow hills, I'll need a car, and a car I will have. I've always been like this when people tell me there's something I can't do: I immediately want to do it.

The doctor then makes a mould of my ear to fit me with a hearing aid. A putty-like substance that then hardens is put into my ear. I am told to come back two weeks later. I leave the hospital feeling a little bit confused. I am not betraying Mammy by telling anyone what she did. It's hard to explain, but it's like no matter what she did, I still don't want to admit it to people. Not to strangers, anyway. That's my business. It's my story, and I don't need to be going on about it to other people. What happened, happened. *Sure, I'm grand now*, I think. I'm away from her, so she doesn't affect me any more. She doesn't have a hold on me. I am living my own life. I'm lying to myself, of course, but then it's easier than to face the truth of what Mammy has done.

Two weeks later I am sitting in the same room, with the same doctor. I am so glad it's the same room. That settles me somewhat. And here it is, my very own hearing aid. The doctor gently inserts it into my ear. It's uncomfortable to say the least. He explains to me that the brain will need some time to get used to it and that initially everything will seem very loud. After a while, the brain will know what sounds I need to hear and what sounds can be omitted. Isn't the brain just amazing? I can't help thinking that, even as the hearing aid makes my ear feel itchy and hot.

He takes it out and shows me how to clean it and change the battery, and the next thing I'm heading home with my brand-new hearing aid in my ear. I feel quite excited about this new adventure. The possibility of regaining some sounds that I thought were gone forever is deadly. Part of me feels a little anxious still. *Will my brain adjust okay, like he promised?* I wonder, even though I can already hear the sounds of the traffic and the clatter of people walking by so clearly.

I've just got a deadly idea: if I'm with someone who is driving me mad, all I have to do is make sure they are on my left side and then just turn my hearing aid off. That is brill!

CHAPTER TWENTY-EIGHT

A TRIP TO THE THEATRE

'VE REPEATED FIRST YEAR AND AM SAILING INTO MY SECOND YEAR, full of new ideas for projects, but as we head into December, I begin to feel a bit unwell, unsure if I need to get sick or eat something. It suddenly dawns on me that I got sick in first year at around the same time. I begin to wonder if this could be some kind of a pattern. After all, Christmas was a time I dreaded when I was a kid. That's when the violence and the drinking really stepped up a gear, with furniture and broken glass all over the place. We did a module on child psychology in class recently, and it was an eye-opener. We learned that babies in the womb can be so affected by the atmosphere outside, like sudden loud noise or aggressive shouting, that it raises their stress levels. Or, if a pregnant woman has a sudden fall and her heartbeat gets faster, so too can the heartbeat of her unborn infant. I think of my younger sister, Noelle, and wonder how she felt when she was in the womb.

I leave the college building and head out to the street. I don't know where to put myself. I just know I need to walk. After about half an hour, I realise that I am walking in the opposite direction to my flat. I just follow my legs. I am heading towards my mother's house, and as I do, I say to myself, *What am I doing?* I feel so disorientated and confused. It's as if, subconsciously, I just need my mammy.

When I get to her house, I ring the bell. I am starting to feel desperate now and scared. I'm feeling really ill now: I'm convinced that I'm going to die. I keep pacing back and forth as I ring the doorbell. I feel that if I stop, I'll collapse. There's no answer. I start to panic and cry. As I walk around the front garden, I throw up. It burns my throat. Oh, please God, let me feel better now. I don't. I don't get much relief from that at all. I must keep moving. I get back on to the main road and half think about getting a bus home. I very quickly realise I can't, because I reckon I'll either pass out on the seat or keep throwing up. *Keep walking, just keep walking*, I think.

Eventually, I'm only a couple of miles from the flat. I have thrown up another couple of times. It scalds me. It's like hot, yellow slime. I am now holding on to walls and railings as I walk. When I get to the flat, I manage to open the door and collapse in the hall. Tom rings an ambulance, and the next thing I know, I am heading to A&E.

The next morning, the nurse tells me that I need to have surgery urgently. The scan has revealed that I have a duodenal ulcer that is really inflamed. I feel quite calm about the whole thing, even after the trauma of the night before. At least now I know it isn't my imagination.

When I'm lying in the operating theatre, counting from 10 backwards, the taste of gas reminds me of poitín. Suddenly, I'm transported to a recent college trip to Galway. We'd rented a few cottages for a couple of days, exchanging boxes of teabags for bottles of poitín with some fishermen, which wasn't a great idea. None of us had ever drunk poitín before, and there was about an inch of sediment at the bottom of the bottles. That didn't put us off, though. I'd say we all had a good mugful each over a couple of hours, followed by a few pints. Apparently, later that night, I was found walking around outside with a mattress on my head. I then forgot how to walk. I was that drunk. Whoever guided me back into the house had to keep saying, 'Left, right, left, right.' They then put me face down on the floor. So much for the recovery position! I woke up in the middle of the night and crawled into a cupboard. That's where I was found the next day. Needless to say, I will never touch poitín again.

When I get out of hospital, I feel so relieved, but unlike the first time, I also feel a little fragile, which is unusual for me. On my first day at home, I go to the corner shop for a loaf of bread. The guy in the shop asks me if I'm okay, and I just start sobbing. I'm still quite sore from the surgery, but I also feel quite down. Maybe I'm right, and being sick at Christmas is no coincidence. The body remembers. I read somewhere that when we experience trauma, it's held in the body at a cellular level. Maybe my body is telling me something that my mind doesn't yet want to understand.

I also begin to feel the absence of my sister Noelle. I can't explain why, because I would have been only a year old when she died, but there's always been a part of me that's missing, and I wonder if it's her. I know so little about how she died, except that it was a cot death of some kind, but perhaps my year-old self witnessed the trauma and still remembers it deep down. I decide that I need to honour her, so I write her a little poem:

LIVING
Small/soft
Thinking/yawning
Sensing/touching
Tasting/wanting
Hearing/yearning
Beating/tingling
Hot/cold
Light/dark
Stretching/loud
Wet/sleeping

Sleeping
And still sleeping
Good night, my love. Keep forever small.

As the days go on, I start to feel like myself again, but it's another few weeks before I can go back to college. Around this time, before I got sick, I started to lose a lot of weight. I went from thirteen stone down to eight stone in the space of five months. I just haven't been able to eat the way I did before. Because of the ulcer, I have to be very careful now with my diet: no fried or rich food, no salt, nothing acidic, no caffeine, no alcohol, no smoking. There I was, battling with my weight, when all I had to do was get an ulcer!

I need to repeat some of my modules, and because I haven't been able to work in the diner since I got sick, I've so little money for the materials I need, like photography paper. I have no option but to avail of the art school's hardship fund. I'm not giving up, though. I've been through too much to stop now. I won't rest until I leave art college with my qualification in my hand, no matter what it takes.

I have to put a proposal together so I can explain clearly why I need the money, and then I need to meet 'the suits', the art school's governors, who will decide whether I deserve it. At the start of the meeting, I feel like a beggar, and I hate it. Then I think, *To hell with it – that's what the money is there for.* I swallow my pride, make my presentation, and they grant my request. I am so relieved. At least now I don't have to worry about having materials for the rest of the year.

That evening, the building's only phone rings downstairs. One of the guys in the flat below answers it and shouts up that there's an urgent call for me.

I run downstairs to pick it up. It's Mammy. Ah, that was clever. If I had known it was her, I wouldn't have answered.

She tells me about this policy she took out a few years previously for me, which she had planned to put towards my college education, and now it's time to cash it in.

I can't believe my ears. She is actually going to help me!

'Would you like to know more about it?' she says.

'Yes,' I eagerly reply.

'Well, you know what, I changed my mind and cashed it in for myself.' Then the phone goes dead.

I put the handset down and go back upstairs. Taking one look at my face, Tom asks me if everything is okay. I just say, 'Yeah, it was nothing important.' I don't want to talk to Tom about Mammy right now, so I go up and slump down on the bed, wondering how Mammy has caught me in the same trap again. I'm twenty-two years old, and she still manages to do it, every time. Her behaviour reminds me of a cat with a mouse. There's the chase, then the catch, then the flipping about of the mouse, playing with it as if it's a rag doll, which raises the mouse's adrenaline. The cat will often put the mouse down and sit back at this stage, looking disinterested in his prey. He'll start to wash himself, giving the mouse a false sense of security. The mouse starts to walk away slowly, and just when he thinks he's out of harm's way, the cat will suddenly pounce. I'm like that mouse, being toyed with by Mammy, feeling that I'm free of her, before she reaches out and grabs me again, pulling me back into her orbit. I hate it, but I don't know how to change things.

CHAPTER TWENTY-NINE

SHIFTING GEAR

I T'S NOW 1995, and I'm a working girl at last. The remainder of college went without a hitch. I put my head down and worked to the best of my abilities. I was dreading writing my thesis, but I really wanted to follow my heart and write about the fin de siècle phenomenon, which had always fascinated me. Fin de siècle, or 'end of century (cycle)', is a term used to describe a mood, an ominous spirit, that can descend at the end of a century. The phrase was used first at the end of the nineteenth century, with its artistic climate, and is often associated with the years leading up to the outbreak of World War I.

My tutors were a little nervous about my choice of topic, as it was quite abstract, and advised me to write something more straightforward. I told them to have faith in me, and I went ahead and wrote it. It earned me an honour. My final report stated that my thesis was highly regarded by the academic staff. Did my seven-year-old self ever think I'd read that sentence in one of my reports? I felt such a sense of achievement, like I had arrived. I ended up getting a 2:1 at the end. I was actually disappointed and contested the result, because I had put so much work into my final year and I felt I deserved a higher mark. My tutor explained that the only reason I didn't get a first-class honour was because the outside assessors couldn't figure out if my end-of-year project was painting or sculpture. I kind of went my own way in the end. I didn't intend to, but I just had so many ideas.

My sculpture/installation involved floor-to-ceiling lengths of clear acetate with words printed on them. They looked like walls that had been suspended in mid-air. This was a tribute to Noelle. Then I made a five-foot-tall, three-sided confession box, almost like a standing-up box of Toblerone. It had three little velvet curtains, barbed wire on the top and print on the outside. Outside, I had built three little wooden pews, and if you looked through the velvet curtains into the box, you would see a meat hook hanging on a piece of fishing line with a little red ribbon on it. It wouldn't take Freud to work out that this piece reflected my experience of being locked into a confessional by my mother.

I was kind of glad the outside assessors couldn't fit me into any particular box. It reminded me of the interview I had where the panel had asked if I was on medication just because I didn't have a common theme running through my art. I didn't want to be the same as everyone else or to have the same ideas – I wanted to be different.

I've been lucky enough to get a job straight after college. You won't believe where the job is: in the very centre for people with intellectual disabilities in which I nearly ended up when I was a child. I'm so grateful to the teacher who found the key to release my potential. It feels so strange to walk along the corridors, my art materials in my hand, and to think about the child I was then, so defenceless. I never thought I'd end up working here. I've set up art sessions for 110 residents with varying degrees of special needs. One lady finds it too difficult to work within a group, and I've battled with the manager to let me have one-to-one time with her. He eventually agrees, and I set up two tables beside each other, one for me and one for her, with paint, paper and brushes. I'll see her once a week, for four weeks.

The first week, I just sit and paint, while she paces frantically around the room. I make sure the room is well ventilated. I always play gentle instrumental music or recordings of the ocean or the dawn chorus. I also put a 'Do Not Disturb' sign on the door. I want to make her feel comfortable and safe.

On the third session, this lady sits down beside me. She selects a brush, dips into a colour of her choice and makes her mark on paper. She then makes eye contact with me for the first time and laughs. This is a magical experience.

I'm also helping a young boy who finds it hard to concentrate. He is quite a challenge, losing his temper a lot and throwing furniture around. I think it could be frustration that he doesn't have the words to express himself, as he's non-verbal. It reminds me of Enda when he was younger. I ask to take this young boy for a few sessions, again, on a one-to-one basis. After trying various approaches with little success, I get a big roll of wallpaper and lay it across the floor. I tape a roller on to the end of a piece of bamboo stick and leave a tray of paint on the floor. He picks up the roller and starts applying it to the wallpaper. After each of these sessions, his concentration seems to improve. He starts to maintain better eye contact, and after a few weeks his teacher tells me that his parents feel that he's no longer as frustrated. Within months, his concentration has improved in school, too. Maybe it's because of my own background, but I feel I can connect with the people in the centre and can see myself in each one of them. I feel hugely privileged to be working here.

I find the work really fulfilling and thrive in the centre, which is ironic, as I might once have been a service user there. I'm writing a diary on my findings in the art therapy sessions. I also give art therapy workshops to various medical students and staff. I stress to the staff that we all need to feel safe and comfortable in our environment in order to flourish. For the staff workshops, I make sure that the room is really stuffy. I close the windows and put on loud pop music. I tell the staff that they are going to be doing a role-reversal exercise: for the duration of the work-shop, they are not allowed to speak, as most of the residents are non-verbal. I then talk very loudly and bang the door open and shut numerous times. I have painting coats, which I button too tightly on to the staff, and I hold their hands firmly, forcing their brush into the colour that I want them to use. Then I paint the picture for them and put their initials at the end of the sheet. Two staff members have to stop halfway through. I invite them to get some fresh air for a few moments and to gather themselves. When we finish, I ask them all for feedback. The common thread running through their comments is a sense of viola-tion and disrespect. Sometimes we just need to be reminded of what it's like to be on the other side.

It's 1997, two years after I started my new job, and Mammy is diagnosed with three malignant tumours of the bowel. She is now sixty-eight years old. The day she is diagnosed and told she will need urgent surgery, she goes to a butcher's and buys a load of meat. Her therapy, I guess. Our relationship is now a strange one. She has bad arth-ritis, so I want to help her with jobs. Not because she's my mother, but simply because she is someone who needs a hand. She can struggle with tasks, such as moving plant pots, painting the outside wall or cutting the hedge. In spite of everything she's done to me, I find it hard to see her struggle with practical things. I would still never trust her, though, not as long as she lives. The thought of her dying doesn't bother me, but I wouldn't want her to suffer. I don't really feel anything towards her: neither hate, nor love. It's just a blank where my feelings should be.

A few evenings later, on the way home from work on the bus, that's when it hits me. It's the evening rush hour. The bus is jam-packed, and people are chatting, reading newspapers and books, listening to music on their headphones. Everyone is in their own little world. I suddenly feel the panic rising. Mammy's been told her chances of survival are extremely slim. A lot of her family members also died from cancer of the bowel, so the omens aren't good. She hasn't made a will, and all I can think of is what's going to happen to Enda. If Mammy dies and the house is sold, where is he going to go? My siblings have young families, and I live in a flat. How do we pay for the funeral? What happens to her house?

Then I think, *How do we even begin to clear out her house?* Mammy has hoarded all her life, and the house is stuffed with old furniture, knick-knacks and everything else she can fill it with. When you go into any room in her house, there's never a place where you can rest your cup.

My head is now a tornado of panic. The next thing I know, I hear Daddy calling my name from the back of the bus. I immediately turn my head in the direction of his voice. Of course, it isn't him, but I immediately feel a calmness coming into my body. I haven't believed in God for a long time, and Daddy has been dead 17 years, but hearing his voice and experiencing that sensation of peace makes me feel that there is definitely something out there.

Mammy is admitted to hospital shortly after her diagnosis. Without hesitation, I decide I'm going to stay in her house – both for security reasons and to keep Enda's routine going. Enda finished in his previous facility when he was eighteen and has been back home living in Mammy's house since then. My siblings have young kids, and my sister Louise is now living in the UK, so it makes sense for me to do it. It feels a bit strange being at home again, but it's easier without Mammy, and once I fill it with my own bits and pieces, I feel more settled.

Enda now attends the same centre where I work during the week. It's lovely to see him every day, weaving his stools, making his rugs and creating pottery. Because Mammy might be dying, and I can't look after Enda full time, I arrange a meeting with his social worker to get him on to the housing list. I know that it could take years before something becomes available, but I need to have something in place for him. I don't know how to explain

Mammy's illness and the possibility of her death to him, so I ask his social worker for assistance with this. Also, I'm really concerned for his mental health. I ask his multi-disciplinary team to keep a check on him over the next while.

Tom is really supportive, as usual, and he respects my need for space at this time. I'm working, keeping Mammy's house going and keeping Enda in a routine. I just don't have space in my head for a relationship as well. In the end, we decide that Tom will come over to Mammy's at the weekends. Enda is delighted with this, as he gets on well with Tom.

The days fly by. We are busy during the day, and after we have something to eat in the evenings, Enda and I go on the bus to visit Mammy. She's doing much better than expected, and soon she's moved to a convalescent home, which means we have to get two buses each way to visit her. Enda wants to see her every evening, so that's what we do: I want things to be as smooth for him as possible.

Honestly, I'm astonished that she's survived, but then, she did say on the way into the theatre that she'd outlive every single one of us. It's strange. In my head, I feel that I'd already buried her and that her death would mark the end of a chapter in my life. I have prepared for her death and felt that I was ready to move on to a life without her in it. Now, I have to rethink everything and I don't really know how I feel.

CHAPTER THIRTY

NEW BEGINNING

FTER A FEW WEEKS MINDING MAMMY'S HOUSE, I've started to look at my life again. It's the first time I've ever really stopped to think about it in great detail. Well, not since I was a kid, anyway. For the last few years, I've been focused on college and work. Now I come to the realisation that Tom and I aren't going anywhere in our relationship. While we are mad about each other and would do anything for each other, I just can't see a future with him. When Tom comes over the following weekend, we talk about this, and we're really honest with each other. He tells me that he's fancied someone else for the last while, but that he was afraid to say it to me.

'Look, you need to start thinking about your own future,' I tell him. I also realise something else that I haven't explored about myself. I start to think, for the first time, about my sexual orientation. I have been drawn to certain females in my life, ever since I was a child. Now I believe I was probably attracted to them. I need to delve into this a bit more. I have a lot of questions that need answering.

Coincidentally, there's a copy of *In Dublin* magazine in the front room, a listings magazine for the city. Flicking through it one night, I notice an ad in the back for a group called First Out, for women coming out for the first time or unsure about their sexuality. This group meets on the first Wednesday of each month. It feels like a sign. I tell Tom that I'm going to go along to the next meeting. He doesn't seem all that surprised and tells me that he supports my decision, no matter what.

The day of the meeting comes before I know it. I stand outside for ten minutes before I have the courage to ring the doorbell. I'm also nervous that someone on the street will recognise me. The fear of being beaten up is very real for gay people. As soon as the door opens and I'm warmly greeted, those thoughts vanish. I go up the narrow staircase and am invited to look through the little library while we wait for others to arrive. After a bit, the coordinator tells me that only one other person has turned up this evening, a woman called Susan. When I'm introduced to her, I know instantly that I'm going to spend the rest of my life with this woman. It's not so much a physical attraction: it feels like more of a soul connection. It is the most bizarre experience I've ever had.

When Susan and I leave that first meeting, we go for a drink across the road. We tell each other more about ourselves, and the more we chat, the more I know that she will be someone special in my life.

After about an hour, I have to go, as I have made plans to meet other friends. We don't make definite arrangements to meet again, and when Susan says that she's going to have to miss the next few meetings due to other commitments, I have to admit I'm disappointed. I continue going to the meetings regardless, and before long I've made friends from the group. We go to gay clubs and bars, and there's even a swimming group that goes to Ringsend pool. My life is transformed. When I'm with these women, I feel fresh, rejuvenated, almost like I've had a chance to start my life again. After so many years of questioning myself, it feels as if I've come home, and even though it's two months before I see Susan again, I make a note of each week that goes by, because I know in my heart that I'll see her again.

Mammy is recovering well at this stage and I'm back home with Tom. I still can't believe she survived the surgery. Because the cancer is hereditary, we all have to be screened now, and it really worries me. To distract myself, the weekend before my colonoscopy, I go to a gay bar housed in a former army barracks. I love the venue. There are women of all ages there, the music is brilliant, and there are pool tables – what's not to like! I have quite a lot to drink, as I'm trying to drown out my fear of this cancer thing. I'm standing in the middle of the dance floor, motionless, aware of all this movement and noise around me. It's as if I'm in some kind of a daze. The next thing, I see this vision floating towards me through the smoke on the dance floor. It's Susan! I have to blink and touch her arm before I can believe she is really there. I'm happy beyond words.

'Look, I'm sorry I'm in such a state,' I tell her. I explain to her about Mammy and my anxiety about the colonoscopy.

She reassures me that all will be well. We chat for a bit, then she returns to her circle of friends, but not before she arranges to ring me the next day. From then on, we are inseparable. I'm upfront and completely honest with Tom the whole time, and I'm very aware of how difficult it must be for him to witness me getting ready to go out and meet a woman. He admits that he isn't completely surprised by the situation and was just waiting for me to realise and then tell him. He knows me better than I know myself. I try to be as sensitive as I possibly can. Tom is so supportive and mature about the whole situation, though – he even asks me about various aspects of the gay world. 'You know,' he says. 'I still love you, Ais.'

I feel the same, but he knows I'm not *in* love with him.

Over the next few weeks, Tom and I come to terms with our new world. Three months after meeting Susan in the barracks nightclub, Tom and I separate for good. Susan wants me to move in with her, but I'm not sure that's a good idea. I need to get my own place for a few months, to get my head around the whole thing. I have been living with Tom for seven years and I can't just suddenly move into someone else's environment. Susan understands, and I get myself a little bedsit. Tom and I make the transition to being friends peacefully. We arrange to meet once a week and agree that our friendship is always going to be important to both of us.

I live in the bedsit for three months on my own, and I really enjoy being by myself. There's a real freedom in pottering about doing my own thing in my own space. Soon, however, I'm ready for the next step. Susan and I move in together to our own rented apartment, right in the centre of the city. We both want to move into a new space together, to start afresh, rather than me move in with Susan or Susan with me, with all of our baggage.

My family are very shocked when I tell them about Susan. I don't think any of them suspected that I was gay, but that's fine. I know we'll all get used to the idea in time. But I just can't bring myself to tell Mammy initially. When I do tell her, her response is predictable. She's extremely insulting to Susan and makes horrible remarks. I'm devastated. Mammy can say anything she likes about me – I've long since got used to it – but her calling Susan names is so hurtful. Still, I continue going over to Mammy's house to do her DIY and other jobs, now that she's back from the convalescent home. I'm torn, because in spite of Mammy's disrespect of my relationship with Susan, she's an older woman who needs help, and I don't like the idea of her getting ripped off by a stranger. The carer in me can't help responding to this need. Susan worries when I go over to Mammy's. I've told her everything, and she's concerned that I won't come back alive. I know that Mammy can't hurt me any more physically, because she's frailer than she once was and I'm a grown woman. Mentally is another matter altogether.

CHAPTER THIRTY-ONE

BREAKDOWN ON THE M50

I HAVE CONNECTED WITH SUSAN IN A WAY THAT IS SO NEW TO ME, and yet it feels like this is what I've been waiting for my whole life. I have fallen deeply in love with this woman. She even shares my dream of living in the countryside. We've decided we'll save really hard to try and buy a house together in Wicklow. If we're living in the country, we'll both need to drive, of course. Susan already knows how to drive and has her own little car, but I don't. This is to be my mission, or at least one of them. Even though the doctor at the Eye and Ear Hospital told me that I may find it a struggle, I'm determined to learn. I've overcome worse obstacles, anyway.

I start driving lessons in the city. I'll never forget my first one. The instructor, Peter, is a lovely guy, but as soon as I meet him in his office in Dorset Street, he escorts me out to the car and tells me to get into the driver's seat. *Hang on,*

I think, *why is he getting me to sit on this side? Surely, he's going to wait until he drives me somewhere quieter.* I get in anyway. He tells me about the pedals and the gears. I still think I'd relax more if we were in a quieter area, but no such luck.

'Okay,' he says. 'You're in neutral, start her up.'

'Hang on,' I say, 'I know absolutely nothing about driving.'

'This is the best place to learn. I guarantee you,' he says. He talks me through starting the car, then tells me to do a U-turn on Dorset Street. I think I'm going to throw up. Then I think, *If we crash, it's on his head.* I turn the wheel as instructed, keep an eye out for traffic and before I know it, I've done it. I've actually done it! I've got the car to move, and I haven't hit anyone. He then directs me to the Phoenix Park, and we continue the lesson there.

Peter's car is grand and small. From then on, every week I start the lesson from Peter's office, and I drive him back when it's over. Every time I feel nervous about a certain manoeuvre, I just think of the doctor in the Eye and Ear, telling me I might have problems learning to drive. This only spurs me on.

After about three months of lessons, I do my driving test and fail. I'm pissed off. The tester brought me to an industrial estate full of moving trucks. I was out of my depth and wasn't sure how to apply the rules of the road in that situation. I failed, he tells me, because I was too apprehensive. No shit! Sitting in a Nissan Micra watching 18-wheelers heading your way can have that effect on you alright. Anyway, I immediately put in for a cancellation to repeat as soon as I can. I re-sit the test, and I pass. This time, I was tested on roads with white lines and signposts on them, which made a huge difference.

Now I need to buy a little second-hand car. I have just started a new job, working for people with neurological conditions, but while it's a permanent position, I've only been there for four months, so it's hard to get a loan. I only have one other option. I have never done this before, but I decide I will ask Mammy for a loan of £1,500 to be paid back in cash, weekly, at the current rate of interest. Our relationship has been stable enough for the last while, so I take the chance.

I'm in Mammy's house, helping out with some DIY jobs, and I notice a new photograph on the mantelpiece. It's of Mammy and a much younger man I don't recognise. *Maybe it's a toy boy*, I think. I wouldn't put it past her. *I'm not going to ask her*, I think as I put away the hammer and screws. It's her own business.

I pluck up the courage to ask for the loan when we're sitting at the kitchen table, drinking tea. I'm shaking with nerves, but I hope she'll understand, because she's always understood pounds, shillings and pence. 'Mammy,' I say. 'Do you think you'd give me a loan to buy a car?' I then go into the calculations I've made about repayment rates and interest, but she cuts me off.

'Go fuck yourself and get it from Susan,' she says nastily.

That day, as I walk away from her house, I decide I need to cut all communication with her for a while. If I don't, I know that I'll continue to suffer. Having the courage to cut myself off from Mammy is very difficult. It's not so much the walking away from her that's the problem – it's the fact that I'm walking away from an older person. I really struggle with that. I have countless nights when I just lie awake feeling guilty. But I need her to respect me as a human being. I'm not going to tolerate abuse any longer.

Separating from Mammy has a huge physical, as well as psychological, effect on me. I thought it would be liberating, but for the first time in my life, I experience panic attacks and I find them terrifying, because I don't know what they are. The worst one happens in a bar with friends. We're watching a match on television. The bar is noisy and crowded. I'm struggling to hear what's being said. I suddenly get what feels like a fluttering in my chest. My mouth starts to feel dry, and I find myself a little breathless. I start to cough and just wave my hand at the others to excuse myself. As I'm heading to the toilet, I'm aware that my heart is pumping more quickly now. I enter the toilet. There's a young woman changing a child's nappy inside. She tries to exchange pleasantries with me, but I can't answer her. I pace around the bathroom, and I'm now feeling nauseous. Jesus Christ, am I having a heart attack?

I have to keep walking. I'm now out in the car park and gasping for air. I can't catch my breath. My heart is pounding against the walls of my chest, and I have to bend over. I can't walk any more. All I'm thinking is, *No one knows where I am and I'm going to die here alone.* Shortly after, I hear Susan calling my name. I'm now on my knees. I'm unable to lift my head, but I'm aware my friends are there also. Susan calls an ambulance. As we get to A&E, my symptoms ease, and I feel embarrassed now that I'm in the hospital. The staff check me over and reassure me. They explain that what I experienced was a severe panic attack.

It takes me a while to make sense of this. I had thought I was having a heart attack, because the symptoms were so severe, but it was simply blind panic. In the months that follow, even though I know now what they are, I continue to have them. I'm not able to control these panic attacks, and I never know when they are going to happen.

About a year later, in December 2000, there's a large family gathering that Susan and I are invited to. I haven't seen Mammy for 11 months at this stage, and this will be our first encounter. The pub that we're meeting in holds huge significance for me, because I've spent so much of my childhood there and because that's where I'd found the trowel that day that ended in a visit to A&E. I haven't been in this pub in 23 years.

That evening, I sit a good distance away from Mammy and just meet her eye a few times. I'm being very cautious with her. It's only towards the end of the night that I pluck up the courage to go over to her and make small talk. It's all very civilised and formal. That's as much as I can expect for the time being.

It's a very frosty night, and as we leave the pub, Susan says that she'll need a couple of minutes to defrost the windscreen. As she's doing that, my eye is drawn to the area at the back of the car park where I found that trowel while wearing my Communion dress, all those years ago. I have such a graphic flashback, and because nothing has changed about this place in all these years, it makes it all the more real. There are the same trees, the same car park, the structure of the building hasn't altered and even the name of the pub is the same. It's eerie and frightening.

As we head for the toll bridge on the motorway, I can feel my blood pressure rising. I can also feel myself going into an uncontrollable fury. I start getting aggressive with Susan, telling her to drive faster, which of course isn't possible because of the frost. Then, I suddenly get into a rage and say that I want to drive.

'Stop the fucking car,' I scream.

Susan tries to reassure me. I start screaming at her again, and she pulls up on the verge of the M50 motorway, just before the toll bridge. I get out and make my way around to the driver's side. She locks the door. I'm now banging on the window demanding that Susan move over and let me drive. (I can't drive, anyway, because I am intoxicated.)

'Susan, I'm going to smash the fucking window if you don't open the door,' I yell. As I look at her, I fully believe that she's my mother. A feeling comes over me like a tsunami. As I watch the traffic, I think that each car is also an embodiment of my mother. She keeps coming towards me, wave after wave of her.

The rest is a blank. I'm suddenly in my brother's house, covered in muck from head to toe. I feel very disorientated. Susan tells me what's happened. She says she watched in her rear-view mirror as I just walked off into the darkness. She got out of the car and shouted my name, trying to find me. Then she rang my brother Sean, who met her on the motorway within minutes. She said she was hysterical.

Eventually, after about twenty minutes, I walked slowly towards them. We all went back to Sean's house, which is where we are now. The enormity of what's just happened slowly sinks in. Sean is consoling Susan, and she's in bits.

'You know, an ambulance passed me while I was waiting for help,' she says. 'And I thought it was Aisling in it.'

My sister-in-law tells me that I need to get help urgently. I agree with everything she says. I can't believe that I put myself and Susan in such danger. I must have gone down the embankment, and that's why I was so mucky. Imagine, I had no jacket on, it was minus 6°, and I didn't feel a thing. Meeting Mammy that night must have triggered it. It felt as if my thirty years of experiencing terror and anxiety engulfed my senses all at once.

The next morning, I wake up and just lie there for a minute in a daze, before everything from the night before comes flooding back. I still can't remember what happened from the time I walked away from Susan to my return to the motorway, but I know that I need help and I need it quickly. My biggest fear now is that I'll hurt someone. I've never lost control like that before.

I remember the time that I tried to strangle Mammy. That only lasted a minute or so and was frightening enough. This incident, and the fact that I can't remember it, feels even more so.

I ring a counselling centre in Tallaght. When I speak to the lady on reception, she explains that there is a bit of a waiting list. She then tactfully asks me, 'Is it urgent?'

'Yeah, I think so. I want to kill someone.'

She makes an appointment for me to come in early the next morning and gives me a helpline number to ring in case I need to talk to a counsellor that night. I have never been so happy to get an appointment in all my life. I can't put a plaster on this any more.

CHAPTER THIRTY-TWO

FORGIVENESS

T TAKES ME A WHILE TO GET MYSELF TOGETHER the morning of my first counselling session. Lots of things are going through my head. I feel anxious about the counselling, as I have never spoken to anyone else in depth about this stuff before, apart from Tom and Susan. As I'm driving into the entrance of the counselling centre, a guy drives out and cuts me off. I suddenly feel residual rage from the event on the motorway. Jesus, it's a horrible sensation. It just comes out of nowhere. I'm thinking, *He has no fucking idea who he is cutting off here. If I wanted to, I could follow him, block him and drag him out of his car.* When I feel like this, it's so out of control. Susan said my green eyes were flashing when I tried to smash the window on the driver's side of our car the other night. I know that I need to get rid of this rage. I honestly believe it's not in my nature. Yes, I'm opinionated and passionate about my beliefs, and I would stand up for anyone who I feel is being harmed or taken advantage of, but blinding rage, no.

I sit in the car park for about twenty minutes before I go in. I start to get a throbbing headache. *Where am I going to start?* I think, then realise that I should start by going in. As I'm walking towards the building, I see people coming out. Some of them look very weary. I wonder if I look like them and decide that I don't. Maybe I don't need counselling after all. I'm tempted to ring the reception, cancel the appointment and drive home. Then I stop for a minute and think: *What am I doing? I've never backed out of anything in my life. I'm the one who made this appointment, and I'm going to follow this through. I'm going to look on it as a gift, from me to me.*

The general atmosphere in the centre is warm and welcoming, and as I wait in reception, I don't feel uneasy about it now. My God, how important it is to have an environment that feels safe and non-threatening. A young woman comes over and introduces herself as Danielle. She brings me into a room that's very simply laid out, which is good. Nothing is screaming for my attention; there's nothing to distract me. I settle myself, and my head is blank. Where do I begin with this?

I start to blurt everything out in a manner that doesn't make sense. The outpouring reminds me of an art movement called Dadaism, which practised free association. The Dada principle was not to plan or think about your idea, but to let it happen by itself. I speak frantically in riddles for about thirty minutes. The first session is an hour long. The first fifteen minutes are taken up with paperwork and ground rules, which just leaves about fifteen minutes after my rambling.

The counsellor's head must be bursting. She intervenes about ten minutes before the end, saying she wants me to try and ground myself before I go back out to the street.

I find it hard to stop talking now that I'm on a roll, but Danielle says she's concerned, because I've started to churn a lot of stuff up. She also says that I need to really mind myself between now and the next session.

At the beginning of this session, I had to sign a contract, which felt weird. It was a real eye-opener, though. I had to agree that, yes, while these counselling sessions are confidential, if Danielle feels that I am a danger to myself or others, she has an obligation to report me to the guards. Holy fuck. This is real.

In a sense, I'm relieved as well. I now have a real responsibility to get on top of this. It reminds me a little about the commitment I made to my one-to-one teacher when I was a child. It was up to me to meet her halfway. If I could do it then, I can do it now. I need to honour that little kid, I decide.

I commit myself to these sessions. They go on for weeks. I talk about many things: my constant anxiety as a child, my bouts of anxiety as an adult and that sense of being in constant fight-or-flight mode. The fact that I absolutely hate surprises. I plan everything meticulously, because as a child I just never knew what was coming next. This frightened the hell out of me, as I had no control over it. I remember during one of the psychology lectures in art college, we discussed whether certain reactions that we have are learned reactions or something we are born with. I remember that example we discussed of the pregnant woman whose heartbeat rose when she fell on a visit to the GP. She was fine, but when the doctor examined her, he found that her baby's heartbeat had risen too. Apparently young infants have an inbuilt instinct to raise their arms to defend themselves against an oncoming danger.

Danielle and I talk about so many things during the sessions. I remember landmarks in the calendar, like Christmas and Halloween, and how they didn't hold any significance for me as a child – and, to be honest, they still don't. One morning, when I was about nine, I was woken by the sound of Mammy coming into my bedroom. My natural reaction was to spring up on the bed and curl into the corner of the wall as far as I could go. She was holding a tray with boiled eggs, toast and a mug of tea on it. She put the tray on the bed and said, 'Happy Easter,' smiled and walked out. I looked at the tray in confusion, trying to figure out the trap. I noticed that she'd painted faces on the two boiled eggs. I then figured out that it really was Easter. While I appreciated the genuine thought and effort that had gone into painting those happy faces, I couldn't trust the gesture because I knew it would be followed by a night of sheer terror.

We discuss my education and how much of it I missed as a child. On reflection, I think that Mammy probably didn't even realise how little I was going to school, as she was working full time and Daddy was generally unwell with emphysema. But I didn't understand why, any time I mentioned anything to do with school, Mammy would lose her temper. I thought at first that this was because she just didn't care, but later, I learned that her own education had been taken from her as a young woman, so perhaps she resented mine. The effect of this was that I never talked about school, trips or any extra-curricular activities for fear of setting her off, and this meant that even though school was a safe haven for me, it was still associated with shame.

I think that my position in the family was also difficult. I came just after my brother Enda, who had special needs, and before my sister Noelle, who died. If she had lived, I'd have almost had a twin, and while we would have fought, I'm sure we'd have been close too. Sometimes I imagine what it might have been like to have someone in my corner when I was a child. Also, Mammy is old enough to be my grandmother, and some of my siblings are old enough to be my parents. My sister Clare is nine years older than me, and Enda is four years older than me, but I find the large gap between the rest of my siblings and me hard at times. They did their best for me when I was a child, but while they grew up in the '50s and '60s, I grew up in the '70s. We literally grew up in different eras. Whenever we get together as a family, we have great craic and I savour the occasions, but sometimes it's like I'm floating in the family tree.

Initially, I'm very angry during the counselling sessions. This gradually turns to sorrow and a sense of loss. I then start to feel resigned to the fact that as long as Mammy is alive, nothing is going to change, except me. With that, I start to feel calmer. But the most amazing thing I walk away with, at the end, is forgiveness, which is completely unexpected. I now forgive Mammy. I don't love her, but I forgive her. It's for my own sake, because I know that, as long as I keep this anger inside me, it's going to eat away at me mentally and physically. Susan's having a hard time trying to understand this, but in forgiving my mother, I have now given myself back my freedom. I feel that the shackles have been taken off me.

CHAPTER THIRTY-THREE

ANOTHER CHANCE

T'S NOW AUGUST 2001. A couple of weeks after the counselling sessions end, I invite Mammy and Enda down to see our new home. After so long wishing and saving, Susan and I achieved our dream of moving to Co. Wicklow. Between us, we just about made the deposit for a new home in a country housing estate, and we queued overnight outside the building site to secure one of the houses. We moved into our home about a year later, and while part of me was reluctant to ever have Mammy in our home, another part of me demanded that she witness the life I've made for myself. I am going to give Mammy another chance.

When I was living with Tom, I bought a beautiful wooden salad bowl and kept it on top of the wardrobe. It was not to be used until I had my home in Wicklow. It was a symbolic gesture. Something to make my dream real. I was never so proud of myself as I was the day I unpacked that salad bowl in the kitchen of my own home in Blessington.

Enda has also moved on. After the last few years living at home with Mammy, he has been lucky enough to secure a residential house that is staffed 24/7, with a group of other lads with similar needs. He's able to stay with Mammy at the weekends. It must be extremely hard for Mammy to let Enda go, and I don't take that for granted.

Today, I am driving to Mammy's house to pick her and Enda up. It's a journey of a little more than an hour. I feel a mix of apprehension and excitement, but when I get there, all seems well. Enda's in good form. He seems relaxed, and Mammy seems quite level as well. She's even dressed and ready to go. As we head off, I feel a lot more at ease, and I'm so looking forward to the day. The weather's dry, which is a bonus.

The plan is, we're going to stop in Blessington for a leisurely lunch and then go back to our house. We'll have a couple of hours there to have a look around and chill out before Susan comes home from work. Then we'll have a relaxed dinner, and later, Mammy can sleep in the spare room, which I've prepared for her. Enda can sleep on a blow-up bed in the front room downstairs. You see, the third bedroom upstairs, I've turned into an art studio.

We get the makings of a big slap-up breakfast for the morning: rashers, sausages, pudding, mushrooms, batch bread… the works, and we set off. As I'm halfway home from Mammy's to ours, I sense a change in the air. Mammy's starting to get a little sleepy and detached. I still don't worry, because I don't smell any alcohol off her, even though I know her drinking habits haven't changed, and she didn't take anything while I was driving. She usually takes a Lucozade bottle full of brandy in her bag whenever she goes anywhere. This, I can handle, as long as she's sober at the start.

We get to Blessington, and I manage to get a really good parking space close to the lunch place. I feel such a sense of pride. She's about to see my little town. I open her door. She steps out and falls flat on her back.

'No!' I cry. Mammy's not moving. She's dead. She has to be dead. The sound of her skull hitting the pavement is horrific. I stand there for a second, expecting to see the blood ooze on to the pavement. Nothing comes. I get myself together. A stranger runs to my assistance and I say, 'No, no, thanks a million, I'll be okay.' I'm now trying to reassure Enda as well, because he's starting to get upset. I veer between shock, fear, embarrassment and disappointment in the pit of my stomach.

Between us, Enda and I manage to drag her up and fold her into the back of the car. The drive back to my house now feels meaningless. Enda's face is flushed, and all I can do is put my hand on his. 'Enda, did you see Mammy take any tablets before she left the house?'

'Yes,' he says sadly.

I'm not surprised. When she's not drinking, she can sometimes take too many Valium.

It isn't quite the homecoming I'd envisaged. Just as I'm getting out of my car, I see Susan pulling up. She's home early. I run over and tell her not to get out of her car. 'Can you take Enda straight back into town for something to eat while I sort out Mammy?' I ask her. Enda has been traumatised enough today, and it's not fair on him. He was so looking forward to this weekend.

Susan understands immediately. She's really good with Enda, and I'm so glad she's able to do this for me. I manage to drag Mammy into the house. I lie her on the front-room floor, because I'm afraid she'd fall off the couch. I roll her on to her side in the recovery position, placing a pillow under her head. Then I leave a bucket beside her, in case she gets sick. I take the Lucozade bottle and empty it down the sink. I can't touch the tablets in her bag because I don't know which tablets are for what. I know she's on different tablets for various ailments. I drape a quilt over her, close the curtains and walk away.

I spend the rest of the night going up and down the stairs, constantly checking on Mammy. I keep holding a piece of tissue in front of her mouth to see if she's breathing. I just feel bunched now, exhausted, but it's strange: I'm reacting quite differently to the way I usually would when she destroys an event. I don't feel angry. Sad and disappointed, yes, but not angry. I feel quite calm. *Maybe I did get some coping tools from the counselling sessions*, I think.

First thing in the morning, I brace myself and go back downstairs. As I sneak in to check on Mammy, I see tablets strewn over the carpet in front of her. 'Shit,' I say. 'She's after completely overdosing now.'

I need to wake her. I gently shake her. 'Mammy, Mammy, I need you to wake up.' She slowly rouses herself. I manage to help her sit up slowly with her back to the couch for support. After a few moments, I get her to the toilet. Thank God there's a toilet downstairs. She seems kind of lucid now. I'm hoping she didn't take any of those tablets.

Susan tells Enda to have a good lie-on and brings him breakfast in bed, because I don't want him to see this. Mammy seems to come around, and I'm anxious to get something into her stomach. She takes some tea and toast. Reluctantly, I sit with her in silence, just the two of us. After a while, she says, 'I'm sorry about yesterday.' I actually empathise and simply say, 'It's okay.' There's no need for me to say anything else.

Susan takes Enda off for a walk around the lakes while I'm getting Mammy's stuff together. I tell Mammy that when Enda gets back, I'll drive them straight home. She nods her head and says, 'Yes.' Nobody speaks on the way back to Dublin. I put on some music for Enda, and when we arrive back at Mammy's house, I help her in with her bag. Mammy just goes upstairs without saying anything. I drive Enda up to his own house. I try to reassure him and tell him we love him.

With all the turmoil in my life, it feels all the more important to celebrate my relationship with Susan. We've been a couple now for four years, and she has been there for everything. We've built a life together, and we decide that it's time to have a commitment ceremony. At this point, it doesn't look as if gay marriage is on the cards any time soon, but making vows to each other is really important.

I always swore that I wouldn't have a wedding, as I had witnessed Mammy ruin all sorts of family events over the years. I struggle for weeks, trying to figure out how to have the ceremony without her. This is to be one of the most important days of my life, and I'm not letting Mammy destroy it. At the same time, as bad as she is, I'm not able to imagine my family there without her. In the end, I make the heart-wrenching decision not to have any of my family there. On the day, we have Susan's family and a small group of friends at the ceremony, followed by dinner at Durrow Castle. We stay overnight, and it's a dream, just knowing that I don't have to keep looking over my shoulder. As heartbroken as I am about not having my family at the event, I can completely relax and enjoy the day.

CHAPTER THIRTY-FOUR

THE CREATIVE LIFE

OVER THE FOLLOWING FEW YEARS, we settle into our home as a couple. I go over to visit Mammy every couple of weeks and do whatever jobs need doing. Whenever I feel the atmosphere change, I just go home. I'm not getting caught up in that trap any more. In actual fact, now that she's copped on that I'm no longer willing to listen to her aggression, she's started to respect me more. She's also asked after Susan more and has started to take a general interest in my life. Mammy knows exactly where my boundaries are now. It's a win-win situation.

I see Mammy in a different light now. She is getting older and seems more vulnerable and dependent, even though she'd never ask for help. I start to ask her how she is, which, initially takes her by surprise. Slowly, she starts to open up and tells me about her fears of being helpless and dying. I sit with her from time to time and let her express her anxieties and thoughts. I ask if she has any regrets in life. She tells me she was lucky enough to be able to do her Leaving Cert, and in those days, that was a rare opportunity. She even got a scholarship to do nursing but wasn't able to take it up because she had to stay at home and work in the family business. 'I resented it, you know,' she says. I can believe that, and I wonder what she might have been like if she'd been able to fulfil her own hopes and dreams.

While these moments are precious, she can cancel them in one swift second, with no going back. She seems hugely mistrustful and must have been hurt herself in the past. It does not excuse her behaviour, by any means, but everyone has their own story. I have a feeling that there's something Mammy wants to tell me, but when the opportunity arises, she doesn't take it. I leave her be, hoping that she'll tell me eventually.

I want to keep maintaining her house for her, as I know how much work she put into it years ago. She knows now that all she has to do is treat me like a human being. Yes, there are times when I get there and it's touch and go at the beginning. I simply start my jobs and talk to her afterwards, by which time she has calmed down.

In the meantime, Susan and I are happily settled in Blessington. We really enjoy our home. Susan is fantastic at sewing and she's been able to make all the curtains, while I've been able to do the DIY. I recently made a cool doghouse. All we need now is a dog to fit in it!

Gardening was something I never thought about before, as I never had my own garden, but I so enjoy working on this one. We've got a garden shed that I've painted purple and I've painted lilies on its glass windows. Now I sit in the shed on an upturned crate and carve wooden pieces by hand. I then treat them in linseed oil. I enjoy the calmness of the activity. In the fine evenings, Susan and I sit in our garden. One bank holiday weekend, I rent out a cement mixer and extend the patio section behind the house. Susan and I then break up pieces of tiles and make a mosaic on the patio. The garden walls are painted white, with large rings made from the copper inside some old electric cabling. We've trained creepers around these copper rings. The garden is our little haven, and we've become quite good at looking after it. We grow various grasses, lavender and bamboo, as well as onions and herbs.

The one thing that does bother me slightly, which never seemed to be an issue before I had my own home, is my obsession with safety in the house. When we were renting, I didn't have this problem, but now that I have my own house, I notice that when I'm stressed or tired, I have to turn on the lights to make sure they were off in the first place. I often put my hand under a tap to make sure it is off, at times even pressing my hand against the spout, so that I see a little ring of water on my hand, as further proof that it is off. Door handles get the most abuse: they are pressed down numerous times. The more tired or stressed I am, the more I check. I also run my fingers over empty sockets to make sure they are switched off. It's really tiring. At times, I just keep checking the same thing over and over. I'm like a hamster on a wheel. I have to give myself at least twenty minutes extra before leaving the house in order to make time for checking. Susan gets frustrated at times, to the point where she just tells me to go out and sit in the car. She will then do a quick check to make sure everything is off. I find that I'm okay once I know I'm not the last person leaving the house.

I remember someone saying years ago, jokingly, that I had obsessive compulsive disorder, but I laughed it off. I didn't realise until now just how true it was, even though I have never sought a diagnosis. My 'To Do' diary is a vital part of me. If there's a job to be done, I write it in my diary and it's done. One year, I even tried to take it on holiday. When we got to the airport, Susan had to prise it off me and leave it in the glove compartment of the car before we got the flight. The idea of not having it stressed me, but we laughed about it once we got on the plane. I find that being creative really eases my OCD. Now that I have my own little painting studio, I've bought big rolls of canvas from college suppliers so I can make my own canvas frames, and I spend the winters painting.

Still, from time to time, I have the temptation to end it all. I don't know why, because everything in general is fine. There's a section of wall along the Liffey in Dublin that's really low, and I know that all I'd have to do is lean far enough to the side, as a large truck passes, to be blown in and drown. My swimming skills are still dodgy. Whenever I walk that way, I always have to make a conscious decision to pull away from that wall. There's also a bad bend on the road home to my house, and sometimes I think that all I'd have to do is let go of the wheel at that very point and it would all be over. However, as the years pass, the urges grow fainter, and I pray that I won't have them again.

Susan and I have really settled into our lives in Blessington. I've became a founder member of a west Wicklow arts group that we called Cruthú, which means 'create'. It's a group that is open to anyone with a passion for art. They don't have to have formal training to join us, they just have to enjoy the process of making art. I was on the committee initially, and the first few meetings were held in my home. I designed the logo, which is used to this day, someone else did the advertising and another looked after the legal aspect. Everyone played a vital part. Before we knew it, we had an arts group.

The group has gone from strength to strength. Through lots of bag packing and other modes of fundraising, we've been able to acquire one of the outhouses in Russborough House to use as a studio. We have to sort out the roof, heating and electricity, which we do over time. During the season, everyone takes turns looking after the gallery at the weekends. It's a tight ship, and it's wonderful to see the variety of arts and crafts on show. A hub of creativity.

I feel so proud of everyone in the group and just love the camaraderie that comes when we meet up together in the springtime to get the gallery cleaned up and ready for the new season. We're up and down ladders, drilling holes, changing light bulbs, touching up the walls with paint and rearranging shelves. The kettle and teabags are never far from us. Did I ever think in my life that I would be part of an arts group set up in the grounds of Russborough House? I feel very proud indeed.

CHAPTER THIRTY-FIVE

AN COSÁN

N 2006, I START TO REASSESS MY LIFE AND WHERE I'M GOING. After reflecting on the benefits of personal counselling and the life-changing effect it had on me, I want to give something back. I decide to do a diploma in counselling and psychotherapy. On my way home from work one day, I pluck up the courage to go into an adult education centre, An Cosán, and see if I can talk to one of the course leaders. I don't have an appointment, and I feel a little cheeky doing this, but I have nothing to lose.

The warm, welcoming atmosphere in that building is amazing. I get to meet one of the leaders, and after a chat she recommends that I apply for the course. I walk away from the meeting in shock. Am I actually going to do this? It's going to be a huge commitment. There are going to be sacrifices, but it just feels right.

The timing could probably be better, but I decide that I need a fresh perspective. For the last couple of years, Susan and I have begun the process of intercountry adoption. I've always had a ferocious tendency to protect my loved ones, just like I protected my inanimate friends, the stones, as a child, and I know that Susan and I will make great parents. But while we're eventually approved by the Health Service Executive to adopt from overseas, it's a very difficult journey – emotionally, as well as financially. At this time, South Africa is one of the few countries that's open to adoption by same-sex couples, but just as we near the end of the process, the country closes its intercountry adoption programme.

With that avenue closed to us, we decide that IUI (intrauterine insemination) might be the answer. However, we can't avail of it in Ireland at this time because we're a same-sex couple, so we travel to the UK. We have to leave home in the middle of the night to catch an early flight and be at the clinic for a morning appointment, have treatment, and then turn straight around to get the next flight back to Ireland, so that we can both be in work the next day. I haven't told any of my work colleagues what we're doing, as I'm extremely private, but we find the process exhausting and gruelling.

During this time, the policy on donor insemination for lesbians in Ireland changes, so thankfully, we're able to have treatment locally. Things are looking up, but after

Susan, who has elected to carry the pregnancy, has two miscarriages, we are down and out again. I deal with the second one quite badly, because I was sure that this time it was going to be a success. We've been renovating an old cottage, and instead of staying at home with Susan, I decide to head down and spend a couple of hours picking out heavy stones and piling them in heaps for no logical reason. Perhaps it's just my way of dealing with the end of our journey to be a family, but I know that I should have been with Susan. My heart is ripped in two.

I often wonder if I would have made a good mammy, in spite of my own upbringing. I like to think that I would have. I always remember that one day, when I was working in the diner as a teenager, a woman was eating her meal with her young child sitting opposite her. The child was no older than five, a little girl. Suddenly, I heard a growling sound, followed by what sounded like a violent slap. I turned as quickly as I could and saw the woman pulling the child roughly by the arm across the table. The little girl had knocked over her glass and spilled her drink. Her mammy was furious. I immediately made my way to the table, enraged at the woman's reaction, but feeling a desperate need to stay calm for the child. I mopped up the spill, stressing to the mother that, 'It's okay, it's only a drink, it's not a problem. I'll get you another glass straight away.' The child and I made eye contact, tears and fear welling in her eyes. I knew that look so well. I also knew that if the woman acted like that in public, there was a good chance the child was being mistreated at home. I wanted to scream from the top of my lungs, knowing there was nothing I could do to protect that child. If Susan and I were to have a child, I know that I'd protect that little being with all my might. But with every day that passes, it looks like that dream won't become a reality.

The counselling course is a revelation. It's 11 years since I was last in college, but I'm in a very different place, in my head and in my body. In spite of the difficulties that Susan and I are facing, I know that we're coping. The course is tough, but I learn a lot from it and hope that my life experience and my skills will help me to be a good counsellor.

It's amazing what's brought up for me in training. All our lives, we encounter individuals who trigger all sorts of emotions and reactions in us. Most of the time, we don't even know why we are feeling frustrated, upset or angry. Our discomfort is often not registered at the time of the event, but it usually escalates later, to a much larger scale, just like mine did with the incident on the M50. When I start the course, I realise that I have a real problem with one of my fellow students, who reminds me so much of a male abuser I knew, in both looks and mannerisms. I am flummoxed. On the second day, in private, I decide to tell the student how I feel, as this could cause tension between us later, and it would no doubt cause him a lot of confusion. He wouldn't have any idea where this tension was coming from. He's really understanding, and I feel so much better getting it off my chest. This student and I connect much better from then on, now that the elephant is out of the room.

When I started this journey, I thought that I could take on a lot more clients than I actually do, but I've quickly realised the importance of pacing myself. As a counsellor, I have an ethical duty to look after my own mental and physical health. I know it won't be possible to be present for a client if I'm not looking after myself. Having said that, I get extremely tired before Christmas 2008. I'm working full time as an activities worker and carer in a nursing home, as well as seeing clients for clinical practice, going for regular supervision in the evenings, attending college in the evenings and weekends, and also doing assignments. I begin to feel that I'm losing myself and know that I have to take better care of myself. I now feel that the simplest of household tasks, like cutting the grass, is a mission, and I've forgotten how to engage in ordinary chit-chat. There's also the temptation to overanalyse everything, when in actual fact sometimes things just 'are'. I take up walking again during lunchtime at work and quickly start to feel more energised.

I believe that counselling and psychotherapy can be a lonely profession at times. While it often strikes me how much laughter there is in my workplace, the counselling setting has a much more solemn atmosphere. Not many clients come to therapy because they're happy!

Susan is so patient while I'm doing the course. She encourages me every step of the way. Initially, I think that if I can manage the diploma, I'll be delighted, but then I grab the bull by the horns and go for the degree. In 2010, I receive a Bachelor of Science degree in Counselling and Psychotherapy. The course is accredited by Middlesex University. I can't believe that I've made it, and when it's all over, life slowly resumes. It's lovely to have some spare time again for the simple things in life. For the first time in four years, Susan and I are able to do something together at the weekend.

My family comes down every summer for a get-together. It's great fun. I'll never forget the first year, when about sixteen of them arrived in a minibus, waving flags out the windows. Susan stood there with her mouth open. She only has one brother, who lives overseas with his wife and kids. Susan's not used to having a family that's so full-on!

When I went for counselling as a teenager, for the children of alcoholic parents, I wasn't ready to speak. When I went later, after the M50 incident, I was ready to go. It takes so much courage to go for counselling, and I can honestly say that it saved my life. It's a raw journey, and I had to meet the therapist halfway, but the session was mine, and I had the therapist's undivided attention. It was a sacred space, a safe place for me and me alone.

My OCD is still, and always will be, a work in progress, but it's certainly not as bad as it was. Once I started to accept myself, I became less hard on myself and less anxious. However, while going for counselling was a huge help, the events that brought me there in the first place will never, ever be erased or forgotten. Counselling does, however, make the world a less scary place to be in. It has also helped my relationship with Susan. She and I had some really bad arguments in our first few years together. These arguments went on for days. Susan hates conflict of any sort and would never fight her corner. I have to admit that I almost looked on this as a weakness in her. It reminded me of Daddy and the way he very rarely tried to defend himself against Mammy. One day, though, Susan did stand up to me, and it was as if she had found her voice. The arguments became less frequent. Now, whenever we do have the odd argument, it lasts no time at all, and then we just laugh about it.

As my knowledge and experience in counselling begin to deepen, I take on another role at work, that of 'support contact'. If anyone feels they're being bullied or harassed in the workplace, or has had a complaint made against them, they can contact me for help and advice. I get calls from anywhere within the Dublin, Kildare and west Wicklow areas. When I first started this voluntary job, workplace issues could be quite easily resolved, but the problems in the last few years have been a lot more complex. I have to say, if I didn't have my counselling training behind me, I think I would have given up the role a long time ago. But then I'll get a call from someone in need, and I'll be so glad that I'm there to help.

It's my job to clarify exactly what is bullying or harassment for the client. Sometimes I find I have to encourage a person to tell me the whole story. It's often what's left unsaid that speaks volumes. But when a victim makes that call and reaches out for help, that takes more courage than a bully will ever have. This I know from personal experience.

CHAPTER THIRTY-SIX

SELF-CARE

I N THE WINTER OF 2007, we sold our house in Blessington and moved into our renovated cottage. I finally feel at home now. I'm living where I used to dream of living when I was a child.

A lot has happened in the last few years. In 2004, Susan and I exchanged vows in our own commitment ceremony. In 2011, we had our civil partnership recognised in the registry office, and in 2017, I married the same woman for the third time! Finally, gay marriage was legalised, and we are now fully recognised by the state as married, with the same rights as our heterosexual friends. Ireland has come such a long way in such a short space of time.

The first time we got married, Susan and I didn't invite my family, but Mammy was now getting older and seemed a little less volatile, so I wanted to take a chance and have a family celebration to mark our marriage.

Susan and I booked a hotel not too far from my mother's house, so that, in the event she might get argumentative, I could just order a taxi and put her straight into it. Thankfully, the night went without a hitch. Both our families were there, and Mammy was fine. It didn't stop me feeling anxious, but there was great comfort in knowing that her house was only down the road if things got tricky. I was actually glad to have her there, knowing that she could see the life I'd made for myself and how proud of it I am.

As I sit and put the finishing touches to this memoir, Mammy is in a nursing home in Dublin. She's in her early nineties and has dementia and chronic obstructive pulmonary disease. She was also diagnosed with psychotic tendencies on admission to the nursing home. To be fair to her, she managed to stay in her own home until just before her 90th birthday. She had a huge amount of help from Enda, who was able to help her out a lot since he moved back home from his residential facility, and she also had home help. My siblings and I also rallied together to support her. It was a military operation: we'd meet every month to discuss Mammy's situation at home, and these meetings amazed me, with everyone being so respectful. During the meetings, we took turns taking the minutes and not once did anyone speak over anyone else. I learned a lot about my siblings during these times and felt proud to be part of this team.

One of my tasks was to get Mammy's oven disconnected, because she was becoming forgetful, making her dinner then leaving the gas on. I remember sitting Mammy down one day to explain that we would all bring cooked dinners to her now instead. It upset her, but she agreed. It seemed as if life was turning full circle, because as a child I'd turned off the gas when they'd left it on so many times. I told her how much I appreciated her decision and how difficult it must have been for her. I felt really sad, not just for her, but for all older people who have to make these choices.

While in the nursing home, Mammy was diagnosed with Covid-19, which she survived. It's not the prospect of her dying that upsets me, but the fact that she could die with no family around her because of the restrictions. The idea that we, as a family, would have to stand six feet away from each other at her graveside also upsets me. The staff attending to her care needs were all dressed in personal protective equipment, and this was hard for her, because she couldn't see who they were.

Before Mammy got dementia, she told me something that really helped me to understand her. It was the final piece of the puzzle that explained, at least in part, what lay behind her anger when I was a child. One night, when she was still at home, she invited me out for a drink in a local bar. I was praying that she'd behave herself, and when she suggested I get a brandy for myself, I declined.

'I have something to tell you,' she said. I could see that her hands were trembling as she lifted her glass to her lips. 'You have a brother called Ian, and he's the eldest in the family.'

I didn't know what to say. I'd never heard of any Ian. I was silent, utterly gobsmacked.

She nodded. 'Yes, I got pregnant when I was nineteen. I had to leave my home and family and give Ian up. I didn't have any other option. There was no such thing as a single mother in those days,' she said sadly. 'I then came up to Dublin, and that's where I met Daddy.' But now she had found Ian again, Mammy said, and she'd met him.

All I could do was wrap my arms around her and give her a big hug. 'Ah, Mammy,' I said. 'Why did you never say anything?'

She shook her head, unable to answer. My initial reaction to her news was elation: I was so glad for her, and for all of us as a family, to discover that Ian was alive, healthy and well. My joy very quickly turned to immense sadness. This was a secret Mammy had kept for all those years. To think that she could have carried this to her grave, and we would never have had the opportunity to meet our brother. I then tried to wrap my head around the fact that the sister I'd thought was my eldest sibling was actually not my eldest sibling. Ian was now the eldest of the family. I also wondered if

Mammy's sadness and frustration about Ian had contributed to her alcoholism and rage. It was such a pity. *All those buried feelings*, I thought. Life could have been very different if she'd been able to keep him. Tears started to well up in my eyes, and then I started laughing. I remembered the photograph on Mammy's mantelpiece and thinking it was her toy boy. How wrong I had been.

Not long after, a family night was arranged, and I met my new sibling. I felt so privileged to be shaking his hand. I looked Ian in the eye and said, 'I'm your sister, it's great to meet you, brother.' I was shaking with excitement and pride. Ian was welcomed into the family with open arms.

Sometimes, I wonder what life would have been like had Mammy shown love for me. But I know that there's no point thinking like this: I am who I am because of the way in which I was raised, both good and bad. Because of my upbringing, I can relate to others in similar situations, people who have been abused in childhood or treated badly; and because of Mammy, I know that I will never give up if I face a challenge in life. I'll keep on at it. That resilience may have been hard won, but it's there.

Life at home in Co. Wicklow is good. Each morning, I do a little check-in with myself. I sit in the kitchen alone. I watch the sun rising and the birds feeding or flying in and out of the nesting boxes that I've placed within view. I make a big pot of tea and ask myself how I am that day.

Some days I'm okay, but other days, I find that I'm quite distracted or upset about something. I then go through everything in my head until I can pinpoint what it is. Once I know exactly what's wrong, I feel more settled and able to start the day.

Painting remains a big part of my life, and it gives me huge satisfaction. I left the arts group of which I was a member a while ago, as I found it difficult to make time for everything, but I still exhibit locally and transport my paintings in a little van. I always keep a crate and some rope in the back of the van. I use the crate as a step, but you never know, I might just make a swing some day! And I know I'm so lucky to have my own studio. The freedom to hammer away while I'm making my canvas frames is something I never take for granted. To be able to walk away halfway through a job, and know it's safe until the next day, gives me such comfort. When I do start painting, I lose all sense of time. I don't do sketches and never know what's going to appear on canvas until it's finished. I get transported to a different place.

I'm aware that I need to try and keep myself fit, so I do a bit of horse riding in the summer months. I don't have a horse, but there's a riding school quite close to me that I go to, so that I can stay connected to those beautiful creatures. I go hacking with a riding instructor. We go out into the woodland and fields and have a good canter. I always feel so energised after riding, and it pumps my adrenaline like nothing else. It reminds me of running around Murph's field when I was a little girl with my childhood friends. I loved nature then, and I love it still.

Archery is something I took up about three years ago, and I'm completely addicted to it now. When practising, I can shoot a target at 60 feet. I'm part of a fantastic medieval group, and when I go away with them on trips, I slip into the fourteenth century, which reminds me of the dressing up I used to do so long ago, trying on Daddy's tails and admiring myself in the mirror. I still love getting mucky, too. One year I did the Runamuck Challenge with a work colleague and couldn't get dirty enough. It was a brilliant day, and it took me right back to my days of adventure.

Susan and I have a little vegetable patch at one end of the garden, and we grow garlic, leeks and courgettes. We also grow gooseberries, strawberries, apples, plums and pears, as well as herbs. Trying to keep the squirrels away from the strawberries can be a challenge, and the cat always seems to think that my newly dug soil is for his own personal use. We also have a wormery in the shed, and sometimes a couple of worms might fall out when I lift the lid. I pick them up gently and put them back. This always brings me back to the little pebbles in the laneway when I was a child, the way I used to line them up out of the puddle, so that they'd be safe. I feel the need to look after everything, even the little worms, in the way I'd have liked to be looked after myself.

MEETING MÁIRE

OVER THE LAST FORTY-ODD YEARS, I've often thought about my teacher, Máire, the one who gave me Daddy's Mass card and who had helped me with my reading and writing. I used to wonder if she was still teaching, if she had moved abroad or if she was even still alive. In January 2020, I take a chance and look her up. I think I am going to pass out when I find her email address. I decide to write to her and thank her for everything she's done for me. It feels so strange sending that email. Part of me doesn't expect a response. I'm happy enough just to know that she's alive and that I now have the opportunity to thank her. Part of me thinks that she might be reluctant to answer my email, in case she thinks I'm some kind of a stalker, but a big part of me wants nothing better than to meet her in person, to shake her hand and simply say, 'Thank you.'

Within days, I get a reply. I can't believe it when Máire says she'll meet up with me. We arrange to meet in a hotel, as it will be easier to have a private chat in quiet surroundings. As the meeting day gets closer, I have a real sense of excitement, but I'm nervous too.

I arrive at the hotel and settle myself down with some tea. After a short time, I hear that distinctive soft voice behind me greeting the receptionist. I just stand up and wrap my arms around Máire. So much for shaking hands and saying, 'Thank you!'

I honestly wasn't sure how I was going to react when I saw her. I don't cry, which I thought I might, but it's such a joy to have this woman beside me again. Those green eyes are still twinkling, still looking directly into mine, as if she really sees me. I tell Máire my story briefly and about my life now, and she says she's delighted that I've made such a success of myself.

'Do you know, I'm writing a book about my experiences,' I tell her.

Máire looks very impressed, and I say, 'It's all thanks to you. If you hadn't helped me when I was a child, I wouldn't be writing a book. I really want to pay tribute to you in it, by the way.'

'Ah, I did very little,' Máire insists. 'It was your own perseverance that got you through, Aisling.'

'Yes, you're right about that, but you were so kind to me when I was a child,' I say, tears filling my eyes. 'I'll never forget that, Máire. You were so gentle, and that had a profound effect on me.'

That's the thing that blows me away, I think, as Máire and I chat. It's not the grand gestures, but the smallest of things that often mean the most. Just a word of encouragement to someone when they're down, or letting someone know you're there for them, can make the difference between them sinking or swimming. Thanks to Máire, I swam for my life, and I thanked her from the bottom of my heart. Maybe you don't need to be dropped from a height into the water, like Daddy did to me, to decide that you need to swim for shore. Maybe simple, gentle words of encouragement are enough.

Two weeks before I met Máire, I had a session with an astrological reader. I would always be a little cautious of things like this, but she was highly recommended. Maybe it would be a little gift to myself, to learn more about what lay in store for me. What astonished me was that, after hearing just a few details about my life, this woman told me that I needed to write a book. I thought back to Bridget the Traveller, who had read my palm all those years ago and who had told me my lifeline was broken; maybe she was wrong. I can't see into the future, but I do know that my lifeline at the moment is going strong! Up until the day I ran away from home, there were moments when I wanted to die. I found it hard at times to see a future for myself, but I'm so glad that I'm alive now.

It's now March 2020, and I know that I have to get back to the book that I have already started. I need to get it out there, for my own sake, but also for caregivers of young people, to instil in them the importance of looking out for clues that young people might be struggling. Imagine if someone had asked me when I was a kid what was happening? Maybe I wouldn't have told them, but the point is, no grown-up ever did. As I read a chapter to Susan every night, I realise that these are burning issues people need to talk about. These things have always happened, they're happening now and will continue to happen. As a society, we need to break the cycle that can run through families for generations. People should never feel they have something to hide if they've been abused. They have nothing to feel ashamed or embarrassed about.

While I'm writing, I come across Senator Lynn Ruane's book, *People Like Me*, and I find her story about becoming the woman she is today so inspirational. The courage it takes to spill your guts and get something like that out there to help others is so admirable. I am now on fire, so to speak, and think I'll take a chance and email Lynn: perhaps she can advise me on how to get my book off the ground. I want this book to be directed to teachers, teacher trainers, youth workers and anyone involved with young people, and I think Lynn might be able to help.

I get an immediate response. I have to read the email twice. Lynn Ruane has invited me to meet her in Leinster House. I can't believe it. I feel a huge sense of gratitude to Lynn, a sense of pride in myself, and I'm hit by the realisation that this book just might become a reality. As I walk through the gates of Leinster House, I know that my little ten-year-old self would be as proud as punch.

Lynn gives me a warm reception. There is no bullshit. What you see is what you get with Lynn, and I love that in people. She makes me feel very at ease, and I instantly feel that I can connect with her as a human being. Lynn also has a real can-do attitude: she's a true senator. I look at her and see a woman who has survived, just like me. She urges me to get on with writing my book, and I'm so glad she does – it gives me the final push to get it finished.

I'm convinced that there is some kind of divine inter-vention with the timing of this book. I contacted Máire in January 2020: if I'd waited any longer, I probably wouldn't have had the chance to ever see her again, as she was retiring shortly after our meeting. I met Lynn about ten days before the first Covid-19 lockdown and, again, was lucky to meet her before the whole planet was disrupted.

The country has just eased most of its Covid restrictions as I write this, and I can't help thinking about that fin de siècle phenomenon, which I wrote about as an art student. To think that the whole planet is experiencing something like this at the same time is incredible. Mammy has tested positive for Covid-19 but has survived it, just like she's survived everything else. She's made of strong stuff and does not want to leave this planet without a fight.

My heart goes out to those who didn't survive and those who lost loved ones during the pandemic. But most of all, my thoughts are with those kids who have been isolated in abusive households during lockdown. For these kids, school would normally have been some kind of a refuge, just like it was for me. The freedom of sitting in a park or hanging around with friends was denied to them, and I can't imagine what they might have been through. Maybe, some day in the future, one of them will pick up this book, and my story will give them the courage to keep going. You are all in my heart.

I'm still dealing with the fallout from my relationship with Mammy, both physical and mental. I know that I always will be. Sometimes, this upsets me beyond words, but as long as I can breathe, it will never hold me back. I would like to thank my ten-year-old self for sticking around. While I'm driving my little van, I often look at the passenger seat and see that little cheeky face looking up at me. 'Giddy-up, pony!'

ACKNOWLEDGEMENTS

Senator Lynn Ruane gave me time and listened to what I had to say. She put me on track and told me to just concentrate on writing the book. I'm indebted to you, Lynn, for your help, guidance and encouragement. Thank you.

To all those who helped in transcribing, thank you from the bottom of my heart.

To Deirdre Nolan and Sarah Liddy, my commissioning editors, for giving me the chance to tell my story. I cannot thank you enough. Having never written a book before, I was blown away by your enthusiasm and kind words.

To my editor, Alison Walsh. You are a fiercely talented woman. You were able to draw me out gently as we walked along this path together. You made me feel at ease and, most importantly, I felt safe in your hands. I'll cherish the energy of our chats. Thank you for a wonderful experience.

To Rachel Thompson, my developmental editor, for your complete patience right up to the final deadline. Thanks also to Teresa Daly in marketing for your professionalism and vision; and to Fiona Murphy in publicity – thank you for supporting me on the last leg of the journey. And to the whole of the Gill team for making my concept a reality. I never appreciated the amount of work that goes on behind the scenes until now! Thank you for this wonderful, positive experience.

For my siblings, for being the strong people you are. I salute you.

To Karen and Breeda, for reading my first draft and never doubting my quest to get this book out there! Thank you.

And finally to my partner, Susan: thank you for your patience, love, encouragement and, of course, your amazing cooking, which keeps me alive, energetic and well. I also thank you for giving me the space to be 'me'.

RESOURCES

The CARI Foundation provides therapy and support to children affected by child sexual abuse and has a confidential care line: 0818 92 45 67.

The Rape Crisis Centre has a national 24-hour phoneline set up to support adult survivors of childhood sexual abuse: 1800 778 888.

One in Four is an Irish charity set up to support adult survivors of child sexual abuse: 0800 121 7114.

BeLonG To Youth Services is an organisation for lesbian, gay, bisexual, transgender and intersex (LGBTI+) young people in Ireland aged between 14 and 23: (01) 670 6223.

For LGBT Ireland's helpline, call: 1800 929 539.

Samaritans have a free 24-hour number that you can call from any phone: 116 123.

For help with alcohol and drug dependency issues, speak to your GP about services in your area. They will inform you of any self-help/support groups in your locality, along with details about treatment centres or detox programmes and general information about the type of supports that are available.

For more formal supports, each of these organisations have a national database of counsellors and therapists who could help:

- Irish Association for Counselling and Psychotherapy (IACP)
- Irish Council for Psychotherapy (ICP).
- Irish Association of Humanistic and Integrative Psychotherapy (IAHIP)